6-8-2015

Lisa

Joseph
Pat G.
Flynn

2-8-2013

Kissed by My Confidant

CHRONICLES OF THE SILHOUETTE BANDIT

LION JOSEPH P. GRIGGS
&
Isabelle M. Daoud
Ghostwriter

Order this book online at www.trafford.com
or email orders@trafford.com

Most Trafford titles are also available at major online book retailers.

© Copyright 2015 Lion Joseph P. Griggs.

All rights reserved. No part of this publication may be reproduced, stored in a retrieval system, or transmitted, in any form or by any means, electronic, mechanical, photocopying, recording, or otherwise, without the written prior permission of the author.

Print information available on the last page.

ISBN: 978-1-4907-5624-0 (sc)
ISBN: 978-1-4907-5625-7 (hc)
ISBN: 978-1-4907-5623-3 (e)

Library of Congress Control Number: 2015903175

Because of the dynamic nature of the Internet, any web addresses or links contained in this book may have changed since publication and may no longer be valid. The views expressed in this work are solely those of the author and do not necessarily reflect the views of the publisher, and the publisher hereby disclaims any responsibility for them.

Any people depicted in stock imagery provided by Thinkstock are models, and such images are being used for illustrative purposes only.
Certain stock imagery © Thinkstock.

Trafford rev. 04/23/2015

Trafford
PUBLISHING® www.trafford.com

North America & international
toll-free: 1 888 232 4444 (USA & Canada)
fax: 812 355 4082

Contents

Dedication vii
Kissed by My Confidant ix
Prologue xi

Chapter 1	Rosemary 1
Chapter 2	My Childhood 3
Chapter 3	My First Marriage 9
Chapter 4	My Second Wife 11
Chapter 5	Love At First Site 12
Chapter 6	The Project Begins 16
Chapter 7	Final Details 24
Chapter 8	Opening Night 26
Chapter 9	A New Start 30
Chapter 10	Rosemary, My Almost-Love 32
Chapter 11	My New Home 36
Chapter 12	Rosemary Becomes My Confidant 42
Chapter 13	The One-Sided Courtship 44
Chapter 14	The Proposal 49
Chapter 15	The Rumor Mill 52
Chapter 16	One Year Countdown 57
Chapter 17	Final Wedding Preparations 59
Chapter 18	Third Times A Charm (Wedding Day) 66
Chapter 19	Tick-Tock, Tick-Tock As Time Goes By 74
Chapter 20	Learning My Craft 77
Chapter 21	My Education 80
Chapter 22	Lions 82
Chapter 23	Rosemary's Power 89
Chapter 24	Fading Health 93
Chapter 25	Our Pets (Rosemary's babies) 95
Chapter 26	Her Time 98
Chapter 27	The Love I Have Lost 101
Chapter 28	The Ten Promises 103
Chapter 29	Epilogue 107

DEDICATION

This book is dedicated to John D. Daoud and his family for supporting me during my near death recovery.

During one of my episodes when I almost died, John was at my bedside for a whole week. When I finally came to, we chatted for a while. As he told me how I was going to be alright there was a movie playing in the background on the TV called *The Bucket List*. John suddenly had the idea that I should make a bucket list of all the things I wanted to do before I die and we started to gather ideas during the end of my hospital stay.

One of my friends had mentioned that a lot of people including friends in the Lions Club would like me to write a book about my life. John thought it was a good idea and now because of him, this book is finished.

At first I would record my thoughts and John would try to put them to paper,; however my thoughts would wander and were often incoherent as my mind was still healing from my illness. Eventually John turned to his 14 year old daughter, Isabelle, for help. Being a quick typist and having a love of books herself she took the project over.

Lion Joseph P. Griggs

While John watched TV and basically stayed nearby for occasional advice and refereeing, his wife, Monica would make dinner and his 8 year old baby girl would make popcorn as Isabelle and I would worked on the book at the dining room table where John had set up a computer for us to work once or twice a week. I would eat with the family and afterwards John would check over our day's work.

Thanks to the commitment of Isabelle and her father to make sure I got the book done. This book was finally completed three years later and I was finally able to cross off the item that had remained at the top of my bucket list for so long.

During this time Isabel became my ghostwriter. With her help in understanding how a big book layout should be, she made it all come true. Without **Isabelle M. Daoud,** this book simply would not be the amazing piece of artwork that it is. That young lady has proven that she has a firm command of the English language and that she understands what people want out of a good book. I love her from the bottom of my heart as her "Uncle Joseph" as if she was my own daughter.

So in the end of this all, I wish to say thanks to this family and express my appreciation to Isabelle for believing in me and this book. I think in the future as she should completes her education and chooses her life's path in this world, all will see how wonderful and how intelligent she really is. God bless you and thank you.

Kissed by My Confidant

This book was written to help me remember my past after coming out of a coma and dealing with the debilitating West Nile Virus. It's been a major emotional blast from the past. Once you finish reading about our journey through life and experiencing happiness as well as hardships, I hope that you all value what I have come to understand.

With the help of family and friends, you can overcome

ANYTHING.

PROLOGUE

Imagine how it would feel being a prisoner in your own body. You know you're dying; you know you will die. Every day you fight but can't help wondering, today, tomorrow? When? Every bone in your body is always breaking down, crumbling, and there is no cure. Eventually few bones in your body are actually yours, each, another piece inserted by doctors, never to last long enough. You wonder, "Why me?" Some days you spend looking for the silver lining but most are spent with your heart twisted and lurched in knots trying to squeeze out any hope you have left. There is but one anchor in your life, the antidote to your never ending pain. Always in reach but never enough. The one day it truly must save you, you've run out. Nowhere to be found. Hope has run dry, you make the decision. You close your eyes to rest. It's over.

Rosemary had dreams. Some of those beautiful dreams she strived to make a reality on her own. Her other dreams, she enlisted the help of others to make come true.

Rosemary had always dressed like a Hollywood star; with all the jewelry, the makeup, the hair, everything. Her shoes were always open toed, despite her toes being too short, she didn't care. Rosemary's hair was

Lion Joseph P. Griggs

so long it went all the way down to her knees. Her mother would pop in at times and fix it up for her but normally though, Rosemary would wear her hair in a large sophisticated bun. Yet, she would always let her hair down just for me. I loved it.

Rosemary, besides me, was one of the best cooks I've ever known. One special thing I'll always remember is whenever she came to see me or whenever we went anywhere she would slip a note into my pocket with little nothings on it, just for me.

Chapter 1

Rosemary

Rosemary was born in Wyandotte Hospital May 4, 1951. Her family lived in Southgate. Born to mother and father, Margaret and Bartholomew; and had one older sister, Susan. They lived in the same red brick, bungalow house for most of their lives. Until…she married *me*.

An ordinary happy family, they carried on as most do, until one day when Rosemary was nine years old. After school, Rosemary's bus dropped her off. While walking home, she collapsed in agonizing pain unable to walk another step.

After some time Rosemary's mother grew concerned of her daughter's lack of presence and went out in search for her only to find Rosemary sobbing on the sidewalk in gruesome pain – their first ever indication that something was wrong.

Her family spent the next year testing Rosemary trying to determine the cause of her affliction. Was it Lou Gehrig's disease, Leukemia, Polio, or was it Immune Deficiency Syndrome? Which one of a half dozen diseases had sank their teeth into their precious daughter? Rosemary was eventually diagnosed with Juvenile RA (Rheumatoid Arthritis) at age 10.

This began her life's journey as a Henry Ford Hospital patient in Midtown Detroit. Rosemary used varied types of aggressive medications including steroids, injections. Some of the drugs she had taken were experimental drugs used for testing. Rosemary was so desperate for a cure that she was willing to go through wit8h all the unknown dangers of using untested medications to help her stop the disease from destroying the cartilage in *all* her joints and hope for a remission or a partial recovery. Pretty much, desperate for anything to aid her from the unrelenting inescapable pain within her body.

Rosemary went to Catholic schools from kindergarten all the way through 12th grade, graduating from Saint Francis Xavier High School in 1969. She went on to graduate from Eastern Michigan University and every year she began the new school year with a procedure on her joints in either her hands, feet, etc. As time progressed, the disease relentlessly continued to deteriorate and destroy the cartilage in her body. The large quantity of medications she took partially damaged her hearing and eyesight. Rosemary would replace her hearing aids every three to four years. Fortunately, as her condition worsened, the technology to help her improved. The more equipment she used to compensate, the quality of her life would get better. As her case worsened, it seemed as if she could never catch a break. She would overcome one physical obstacle only to have something else go wrong with her. Although she did develop one skill through all of this —thanks to her loss of hearing she mastered the skill of lip reading. All the medications made her so EXTREMELY sensitive to the sun; if she sat outside long enough she would break out in enormous hives.

Eventually, Rosemary could not stand on her own. She had to depend on a wheelchair. Her fingers became so deformed that she could not hold a normal spoon and fork properly. Rosemary would type with a pencil in each hand; she would hit the keys with the eraser ends. She still wrote cursive beautifully and printed even better, despite having to write with the pencil in a fist. As a teacher, when Rosemary taught, she would put a piece of chalk in her fist and write on a blackboard. She loved to teach and to tutor.

Besides teaching, Rosemary loved sewing, singing, the theatre, and, oh yes, me.

Chapter 2

My Childhood

My name is Joseph Paul. I go by Joseph, Lion Joseph Paul, or just JP. I was born in Wyandotte Hospital on February 5, 1953 - 12:30 A.M. on a Thursday, 7 pounds and 7 and a half ounces, 21 inches, and have not died *yet* – thankfully.

My mother and father were born and raised in Tennessee. My father's name was Pink Jr. (1926 – 1987) and my mother's name is Mary Elizabeth (1935 – still kicking). I have six siblings, four brothers, two sisters, and me. In order from oldest to youngest was Philip Lynn (1951 – 2009), Joseph Paul (me), John David, James Michael, Mary Sue, Edward Daniel (1957 – 2003), and Kathy Ann. My mother and father relocated to Michigan in 1952 where my father worked for several General Motors Plants. He retired from Fleetwood in 1982. My mother worked for Fisher's Women's Apparel for twenty five years, at a hotel in Massachusetts for three years, and worked for eighteen years as a home caregiver. She is now retired.

My mother tells me stories about my childhood…unbelievable ones.

Lion Joseph P. Griggs

Mom   Dad

Once, when I was around a year old and she, still a young mother didn't have much experience with fevers. I had an extremely high fever and was experiencing a seizure. She was panicking and couldn't get my fever down, she rushed to the neighbor who lived upstairs in her duplex and the lady grabbed me, and threw me in a snow bank. It brought my temperature right down. It was the beginning of a life destined for trouble.

At around seven years old I went back to Tennessee for the summer to help my grandfather on his farm. At lunchtime, having been in the fields all morning, I decided before we went back to work I would sit down on the veranda and take a break. I rested my legs underneath the porch and fell asleep against the pillar. I woke up in pain and saw a huge spider on me. I screamed a little and brushed the spider away then got up and went back to thinking everything was okay. In a short amount of time my leg began to swell. Grandma used some old Indian remedies thinking it was just a normal old bite; a few hours passed and Grandpa saw that my leg just kept swelling bigger and bigger. When it started turning different colors, he took me into town. It turned out to be some kind of poison from the spider bite. They had to cut open my leg to drain the poison out. Every time they squeezed I would scream and cry; and every time Grandpa would put a quarter in my hand and I would shut up. I loved my Grandfather.

Around eight years old, Grandpa Pinky took me to a stockyard to sell a couple of his calves and pigs. As a farmer he made money this way. I loved to hear the auctioneer and how fast the whole thing went. I was walking around while Grandpa was doing his business, and noticed in one of the pens was a group of goats. One started licking my hand and followed me. It would watch where I went and call to me. Grandpa thought it was funny and cute. He asked me if I would like to have him and I said yes and he said I could take care of him for *Singing Sunday*. *Singing Sunday* was a yearly event when once a year about 50-75 people from the church would come to his house on the farm and have a potluck picnic and sing church songs the whole time. I thought the goat was being invited. I had no idea what was really to come. Grandpa Pinky asked if I had a name for it, I decided to name him Billy – Billy Goat. Every day I would take Billy the leftovers from supper. I would read books to him and talk to him all about what was going on. Billy became my best friend. Everybody would laugh, and always thinking it was adorable. You have to realize that I was a city boy and only went down to the country during the summer so I had no idea what was really going on. After three months, everything was going great. Then, just a few days before *Singing Sunday* came around Grandma looked at Grandpa and told him it was time. Grandpa grabbed his shotgun put his arm around me and walked me out to the pen. He said,

"Well, this is the part of life you need to know about." He put me up on a post with Billy on the other side of the yard. Grandpa took one shot and Billy hit the ground. I screamed mortified,

"GRANDPA!!!!!! What are you doing!??!?!?" Grandpa replied,

"You were raising Billy for *Singing Sunday*, right?"

"But Grandpa! I never knew we were gonna eat him!" I ran to my Aunt Dimple and told her what happened. She told me,

"Well, Grandpa told you it was for *Singing Sunday*." I got mad at myself for not understanding because I thought the goat was my pet. I stayed up in the attic all day looking out the window while everybody ate my goat...they said it was good. I do miss that goat.

I remember when Grandma used to kill chickens for dinner. She would take it by the throat and swing it around until SNAP, its neck broke and it'd be dead. I was scared of Grandma, beside the chickens, she swung a mean switch. I loved her cooking though because Grandma made the best biscuits in this world! Yummy!

Around nine years old, I would play army with the boys in the woods at the end of the block. One time I went charging into the woods I fell and hit my head on a log. I hit it so hard it cracked open to reveal a bee hive. I was face first in a bee hive. Face first! The kids got me home and my mother first gave me a whipping for sneaking off to the woods then got me medical attention.

When I was 10, my mother caught myself and 14 other neighborhood boys in the yard eating her green plums. She got us all out of the tree and told us kids if we'd stop eating the green plums she would make each of us a pie when they ripened. We promised. When the plums were ripe enough, my mother had 15 boys meowing at her door for her pies. She had hoped we had all forgotten by then, but when it comes to pie and boys that would NEVER happen. So, knowing there was no way to get out of it, she got to work. She had A LOT of pies to make. The next day she had my father turn on the TV (TV was new back then) and we got to watch TV as we ate our plum pie reward.

At 11, I started washing dishes for the local diner, did paper routes, and other odd jobs. I fell in love with money – good to have. My father wouldn't buy us clothes that we liked so we earned money and bought them ourselves. I began getting into art and trying to make my own artwork around this time. My father thought my art supplies was a waste of money so I had to buy them myself too. I *really* started getting into being an artist. I wanted to be one – bad.

From 12 to about 14, I was the smallest kid in the class, skinny – very skinny. I thought my brother Phil was super cool because he was a foot taller than me. When he became a greaser I became one too. The only thing was he didn't like having me around and so I got beat up all the time.

By the time I was 13 and came back home from spending the summer in Tennessee, everything had changed. Everybody had become hippies. The greasers always wore black or white with their wallets on their chains, the new style was wearing bellbottom pants, looking grungy and being a flower child. So all my greaser friends suddenly were hippies after only one summer! Everyone had something to say about the Vietnam War. I was ten minutes away from going to Woodstock with some friends but my brother Phil convinced me that I would only get into trouble. That was the sixties. It was a very great time for artists of all kinds, and I had really gotten into psychedelic paintings. After this period of time, I stopped really worrying about my appearance other than when I went dancing.

During my teenage years, my father and I didn't get along as easily as it once had been. My mother said she had married so young that she had never gotten the chance to have fun. I would always tell her when there would be a school dance and when there were dances at the band shelters, blocks from my house. She'd tell my dad that I had gone to bed early and once he was settled into bed watching black and white TV, she would come to the basement (my room) and help me climb out the window and make sure to leave it open so I could sneak back in. My father hated anyone associating with women unless one was going to get married because he thought it was the devil's work. When I came home, my mother would always ask me if I met somebody that I liked or had I learned any new dances? Sometimes she would even ask me to teach her a few moves. I sometimes think that my mother would have liked to have gone dancing with my dad. My favorite thing about dancing was that it was a perfect way to meet girls who wouldn't normally talk to you. Back then, they would dance just to dance. The hardest thing about dancing as a teen was we went from the fox trot to disco dancing. By the end of disco, dancing was only for weddings and certain parties or the theatre. That's why I started working in the theatre in ninth grade. The three things in my life that interested me as a teenager were art, cooking, and dancing.

Going on 14, I had my very first kiss. She was a girl from school and we were working on math together. She lived about eight blocks down from me. Her mother invited me over to do some homework with her, and also gave us permission to play pool afterwards in the basement. The girl's nickname was Pumpkin. After finishing our homework she invited me downstairs where her mother gave us sandwiches and pop. When we were alone for a bit she asked me,

"Have you ever?"

"Have I ever what?"

"Ya know, ever kissed a girl?"

"Not really. Wait, you mean like a girlfriend."

"Yes...would you like to?"

"Yes," so she leaned over and kissed me on the lips. We started making out. Her mother startled us when she yelled down,

"It's too quiet down there!" Pumpkin told me to grab a ball and roll them down the table so the balls would hit each other as we were making out so her mother would hear the noise. Eventually, her mother got wise, and came downstairs snagged my ear.

"Young man, it's time for you to go." Pumpkin wasn't allowed to see me anymore but what a way to start.

At 16, the high school drama teacher, Mr. Lee, taught me how to do prep work and paint sets for the plays. He eventually gave me a part in the show, the "Sandbox". It was a comedy about people that would take their family members to the sandbox when they were dying. The part called for me to stand on a perch about three feet up in a pair of swimming trunks. I was so skinny that they painted muscles on me. In the show, they would bring a people to die and my job as the angel of death was to kiss the boys on the forehead and the ladies on the lips. I would come down for some lines and then I would go back onto my perch and everybody would laugh. When I had to kiss this one girl that I happened to like, I got down to kiss her but I would turn red and couldn't do it. Everybody laughed but Mr. Lee said I was going to have to practice. Up on the stage hung a white curtain, he said to go back there and practice. Everybody started laughing again. The girl I liked was getting ready to start college the next year and I was *much* younger. Anyway, we went behind the curtain but as she was teaching me how to kiss her, everybody could see our silhouettes it earned me the nickname 'The Silhouette Bandit.' The next day in class everyone had heard about the silhouette bandit. When I went for rehearsal the next night, four girls came with her to show me how to do the part 'right.' It was a loooong time before I lived that down – thank God for summer vacation.

When I was seventeen I became a cook for the Wishing Well Restaurant and the House of Barbecue. Then I was the prep cook for a small restaurant called Biffs. I also would work as a caterer for weddings. None of the jobs were full time and I wasn't very good at school. I decided I'd have to start working more hours to make money to buy a car if I ever expected to make anything of myself.

CHAPTER 3

My First Marriage

Due to my illness, I struggle to remember my first two marriages. What I do somewhat remember, best I can, is what follows. One of the waitresses I worked with at Biffs wanted to set me up on a blind date with a friend of hers. We were to go on a double date with her and another cook from a donut place nearby. Our plan was to take the girls out for dinner and afterwards go to the Shrine Circus. We had plenty of laughs and had a great time. The next day was slow at work so my waitress friend called my date from the night before to ask her how she liked me and our night out and then surprised me by handing me the phone. We talked about how much fun we had and wanted to make plans to go out again. The only problem was I didn't have a car so we couldn't go anyplace. Luckily, she had a car and offered to come and pick me up instead. We hit it right off, but she admitted to me that she had someone she cared dearly about in the service. I told her it was okay and that we could stay friends and just hang out. We ended up getting closer than expected and spent a lot of time together. Without meaning to we fell in love. After about 18 months we ended up getting married. But we started out too young.

At this time, I had started going to school at Wayne County Community College and started taking all the art classes I could get while doing odd jobs.

Then almost immediately we had my only child, Buffy. Buffy was the apple of my eye. We did everything together. My fondest memory is from when Buffy and I raised rabbits as a hobby. It was my job to feed and care for them and it was her job to hug, love, and play with them. In fact, the only pictures I have left from that era are of Buffy and the rabbits.

After Buffy was born, my 1st wife wanted to have more children. More children meant even more responsibility. I would've had to quit my classes and work around the clock to support a growing family. Our arguing started to build. As time progressed it became clear that our life goals and interests were heading in two different directions. Eventually we couldn't agree on anything. After approximately five years of marriage, it was apparent that I could no longer remain with my 1st wife, and still pursue my dreams of becoming an artist. I left.

In retrospect, I feel that I wasn't ready for marriage. I did not yet have the maturity to handle all that responsibility. I felt as if I couldn't do anything right in the relationship. Everything around me was imploding. I simply had to move on.

I knew walking out the door that I was also going to lose my father-in-law who was more of a father to me than my own father was. He taught me all about building, keeping things to code, repairing the house, and fixing cars. In a sense, he taught me a trade. I've always regretted destroying the father-son relationship bond with the man I respected most in my life But I knew the trade off and I made my decision.

My relationship with Buffy was so very important to me. I managed to maintain my relationship with her for the next 10 years until the three of us had a falling out and I gave them the space I thought they we all needed.

In conclusion, the best part about my first marriage was my daughter Buffy. I love her dearly and I wish with all my heart that I could go back in time and make up for all the years lost. Since that could never happen I make do with what I have now, which is the fact that I have her back and won't ever let her slip away again.

Chapter 4

My Second Wife

A few years later, I met the girl who would be my second wife at the Ponderosa Steak House in Lincoln Park. It was close to where my 1st wife and Buffy lived. During my visitations, I would pick Buffy up for lunch and we would go there. "Gidget", as I affectionately called her, worked at the restaurant and would help me with Buffy. Buffy and Gidget were like best friends. Well, we got to know each other and one thing led to another. We used to sit in another restaurant after I'd drop Buffy off at home and talk about our life's problems. We became good, then great friends. But once again I rushed into something I wasn't ready for yet. On the rebound, we dated for only a short time before I asked her to marry me. It lasted for only a year and a half. I'm sorry that it didn't work. I have only seen her a few times since.

I wish her all the best in the world.

Chapter 5

Love At First Site

After my divorce from Gidget, I realized that when it came to the matters of the heart I could be talked into anything by anybody, including myself. Therefore I decided that I would start completely over, and I decided to go back to my artwork and give up on the whole idea of any serious relationship for a *long* time. From this point on, I was determined to become more responsible about paying my bills, trying to maintain my relationship with my daughter, and start a new life.

At the same time I was hoping to go back to school for self improvement classes and art; with the full intent of someday graduating and becoming a recognized artist by my peers. In addition, I understood the fact that I needed to save money. So, my late brother Philip and his family rented me a room to help me out, knowing that I needed time to get back on my own two feet.

I was ready to go back to working at Fleetwood but I had decided to go back during model change at the plant for next year's cars. This is when they change the models of the cars by re-tooling and setup for the new design. So it would be a couple of weeks before they would bring back the workers.

I was laid off and my brother said I was sitting around the house too much. Not long after, he saw a sign on the Wyandotte Community Theatre door window, which advertised for the play, *"Stop the world, I want to get off."* It read that they needed a set builder who could read instructions and blueprints.

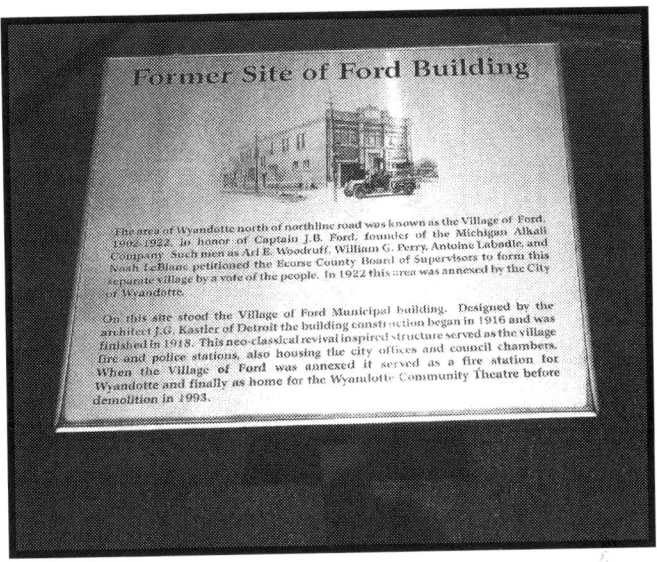

Historical Plaque at the Wyandotte Community Theatre

The next morning I went up to what was called the 'loft'- the home of the Wyandotte Community Theatre.

The loft was the location where sets were built and performers rehearsed. It almost resembled a clubhouse.

I entered the building and went upstairs into the meeting room to ask about the job. A gentleman in the blue room instructed me to go to the main office and speak to a lady named Rosemary who was one of the people in charge of the summer theatre.

I walked around the corner following the man's directions and came to a door. I approached it and peeked through the glass. That was the first time I ever saw Rosemary, a blonde haired beauty who looked just like a teacher that I always wanted to have in school. I opened the door and walked in. She stood up and offered to shake my hand, which was the first time I saw how deformed both her hands were.

She started tacking papers on a cork board as we conversed. Rosemary happened to be using push pins. I noticed that she couldn't get the pins to go in properly. At last, I reached over put my hand over hers.

"I think you could use a little help."

She stopped and looked me in the eyes. After a long pause, she notified me that there was going to be a meeting in the next room in about five minutes and that I should attend.

I went into the room and met all the people. Afterwards, I looked at the drawings and blueprints,

"It looks easy to me but, I don't have any tools right now."

Some of the members lead me to the garage. Inside, it had all the tools and materials necessary for me to build the set. I was told it had to be all done and ready to move in four weeks time. I quipped that I could get it done in two - with some help. Rosemary informed me that she would have to call a board meeting to okay everything and then she would make sure that once we were approved, she would see to it that lunch would be prepared for us every day. Everything went fine and I had agreed to do it. It seemed like a great deal.

Once the meeting was over, Rosemary suggested we go out and get a bite to eat. I was okay with it, but I had no money with me. She said that it was alright and she'd take care of it. The restaurant was a block down where we talked for about an hour.

As it came closer and closer to the time to pay the bill Rosemary noticed that I was getting nervous. She asked me what the matter was. I admitted to her that I'd never had a woman pay for anything. She smiled and shrugged,

"Alright."

She slipped me the money under the table, winked, and said

"No one will know."

I paid the bill. We got up and headed back towards the loft. On the way she tripped on a crack and almost fell. I grabbed her arm and rescued her from falling. We walking arm in arm all the way back to the theatre. The next thing I knew we'd been together talking for twelve straight hours about theater and my life as an artist.

I told her about my family coming from Tennessee; how we were Hines 57 yet we considered ourselves Irish from the McGrigger clan – this is not proven. My immediate family came from sharecroppers in Tennessee and I would work in restaurants as a cook to earn money to buy paints. My life was truly dedicated to my artwork. Even though I knew that I might not make any money off of it and my failures in life were because of my commitment to being an artist.

I also confided that I knew I could not make enough money as an artist so I worked in the factory at GM and would always take classes so I could be a better artist and one day find my way out of the factory life. By that time we were sitting on the front porch of the loft. That's when she revealed that she could see herself being married to a man like me. I replied that I'd already had been married twice and failed miserably at both. I didn't think I was very good in relationships, with families and children. Rosemary just grinned at me and declared,

"Joseph, you're just a 'husband in training' and one day you'll get it right".

Our friendship began from that point on.

We strolled back to the restaurant and had a few appetizers and a couple of drinks. I had a rusty nail and she had a white Russian that's when she told me about her being Hungarian. Her father and mother were first generation from Hungary. She continued to tell me about her work as a school teacher. When we both went to stand, she once again handed me the money under the table and winked. She leaned over playfully, and whispered in my ear,

"Now you owe me."

We got up from the restaurant and headed back to the theatre to go home. It was around one in the morning. I walked her to her car and opened her door. She gazed at me, reached over, and gave me one big kiss.

"Joseph, I'll see *you* tomorrow. I'll call you."

She reached into her pocket and pulled out a napkin. It said, 'thank you, - Rosemary', her phone number, and her address. It also read 'call me anytime.' I watched her drive away and all I could think to myself was

'Whoa, what was *that* all about?'

Chapter 6

The Project Begins

Nine AM the next day Rosemary called. She said the board of the theatre group is going to have a meeting on Wednesday (tomorrow).

"If everything is a go we can start on Monday. Oh, by the way what are you doing this weekend?"

I told her I planned on going to Elizabeth Park in Trenton to paint Saturday and Sunday. I also mentioned that I heard there was going to be a dance in Dearborn on that Saturday night. Rosemary then asked me,

"Do you like to dance?"

"I try," I said.

"Oh, would you like company?" she replied.

"Sure, but I don't know what time I'm going to stop painting."

"Well, I can go as long as you put me in a place that is not in the sun."

"I know just the place. It's a beautiful pavilion and the flowers in the neighborhood are blooming next to the Detroit River. I hope to finish this painting in time for a friend who wants to give it as a present."

"Where *are* all your paintings?"

"I never keep them."

"Well, how can I see them?"

"There's a Big Boy restaurant in Lincoln Park that hangs all my work that isn't spoken for. That's why they're always gone. Tom and Pat own the restaurant and they love my work."

"You're lucky to have such good friends. So, what time should you pick me up?"

I chuckled, "It might be better if you pick me up, my car isn't very nice for a lady like you."

We didn't speak again until Saturday. She called to find out what time to come and get me and I had told her between ten and eleven. She arrived at ten on the dot. My brother, Phil and his wife, Rose were at home. Rose was looking out the window when Rosemary pulled up. One of them teased,

"We thought you went to the theatre to get a job we didn't know you were going to get a girl too." I told them that that's Miss K, the school teacher, and will probably be my boss for the shop. Phil's wife said,

"Boy, do you move fast."

"It's not like that, we're going to talk about what she wants me to do and she's going to watch me work. I think she's making sure I know what I'm doing or checking on me to see what I'm up to. And by the way we're going by her mother's before we go out dancing so I'll be home late tonight."

We went to the park. She had packed a scrumcious lunch and said to me,

"I'm not too sure what you usually like so I hope that this works." I did notice she kept worrying about the sun. Rosemary loved to make finger food. She had made up cucumber salad and stuffed tomatoes with tuna fish, which was really, really good. And some kind of small finger sandwiches and something that looked like trail mix but homemade. Rosemary only drank hot tea, Pepsi, and water.

I set up my easel and started working. She tried to talk to me but it would distract me from my work; she soon realized that art was very serious to me. And she liked it. I started telling her how I tried to paint a picture of water by making the water as transparent as I could so one could see the depth of it. She told me she could see the two point perspective that I used and how I made shadows when I would go to the sky of the picture so in the background one could see the flowers and the stream coming from the park with the bridge as the focus point.

"Do you come here often?" she asked.

"Every chance I can." I sighed.

"Do people come up and offer to buy your paintings?"

"Oh yes," I said. "I make enough to pay for the paints and keep going. I won't get rich but it makes me happy. Some people call it a hobby, I call it my life." As we were speaking, she asked if I liked sports. I told her no. I asked her if she like sports and she said no.

"Good, we'll get along then," she said.

"Although I do like to go see the games live I don't like to play because I had badly broken my ankle when I was young and couldn't play sports again."

"Well, you know why I can't play."

I mentioned how I didn't understand how people argue about what a player should've done when they themselves couldn't have done it anyway. I didn't see the point?

"It's about 5ish and my mother is expecting you. I told her alllll about you last night. Just be ready to eat."

When we arrived, oh my goodness! Her mother acted like I was the son she never had. Her father was the gentleman that I would one day like to be. Their family was one of those families you would see in the Saturday Evening Post, the perfect family. That's what they had…that's what they were. Her mother would never stop feeding you, most of it was homemade Hungarian food – my god, was it good. After we were there for about an hour and half, I said,

"Umm, Rosemary, do you still live here?"

She was like… "yeah" in a 'duh' tone of voice. She looked at me surprised. I was thinking to myself…27 and still living at home? Rosemary got up and went upstairs for something. Her mother came over and gave me another cup of coffee and whispered,

"I think she likes you." Then she smiled.

Rosemary came back down with a real pretty dress on and asked,

"So, what do you think?"

"It's beautiful!" I responded.

"I made it. I make most of my clothes. That's what I do at the theatre." I was looking at her hands thinking how on earth can she do that? Then I realized she must be a very determined woman.

Kissed by My Confidant

Rosemary then mentioned it was time for us to go. She gave her mother and father each a kiss and gave me a look that said get out the door! I scrambled outside after saying my goodbyes and opened the car door for Rosemary. I shut it and then got in, myself. Rosemary looked at me and then smiled,

"Sorry – but I think my mother likes you and she was going to tell you the story of my entire family that never ends and, well, *I* want to spend time with you tonight."

We went dancing. I knew two clubs that still had real dancing. We went to a place that I knew first. Then Rosemary had an idea.

"Joseph, I know a place where all the dancers from the theatre go."

"Really? Let's go." Rosemary gave me a big smile. Most of the people were her friends and were either professional dancers or people who danced their whole lives. I was out of my league. I got up with her for a slow dance. I did ok but I was still feeling extremely awkward and clumsy compared to all the grace and poise that surrounded me. I was watching people who could really, really dance. And I kept thinking,

"What the hell am I doing here?" When everybody went to sit down we ended up taking a bunch of small tables and put them together with about 20 people I'd never seen in my life. Some were singers, others were dancers but most were from the theatre and they were so happy that I was building their set. I realized then, though, that these were people I don't ever meet in my line of work at GM. We had so much fun and Rosemary never stopped looking at me. Her friends kept pulling her away to ask her about who the new guy was. After a while a guy came up and he was sort of rude. He asked Rosemary to dance. She looked at me to see if I minded.

"Sure, go ahead its fine," I reassured her. They looked amazing together. I was asking myself if I'd ever really be able to dance like that.

They actually danced a couple of dances. He seemed slightly flustered and kept talking into her ear while shooting daggers at me. I was beginning to think they had some history together. He brought her back to the table. I could easily see that she had gotten uncomfortable. He gently sits her down then turns to me and in so many words pretty much had the nerve to tell me she was out of my league. He then sauntered off to the bar where he was murmuring and glaring at Rosemary and myself. Rosemary looked extremely uneasy while glancing back and forth between the two of us. I didn't think she wanted me to know him.

Finally I had enough. I felt like some kind of third wheel on my own date! I turned to Rosemary,

"I'm going to get a beer from the bar, can I get you anything?" She asked for a Pepsi. On my way, this same ridiculous guy walks over to me, turns his nose up and sneers down at me and vulgarly said he heard from his friends that I was just some factory stiff that could work with tools. I retorted,

"Beware the guy that fixes your car because I'm the guy that builds them and we are the same. I can put a house together tooth and nail. What can YOU do?" This bantering went on between us for a couple of minutes before he stepped over the line. I finally had *enough* of that wimp. I grabbed him by the privates and hauled him up the wall and snarled,

"Rosemary is with ME tonight. You leave her the hell alone," I then dropped him to the ground, patted his cheek, and brushed off his shirt.

"Now, would you like me to walk you to your car?"

His face had long turned red with fury, humiliation, and pain matching the hair on his head and the freckles on his face. He stormed off. I don't know if Rosemary ever saw him again. But I know I didn't.

I cooly walked back to Rosemary with our drinks. She looks up at me trying to hide her smile.

"For the lady," I said as I handed her a Pepsi.

"What was all that about?" she asked. I replied,

"I think it was about you."

She just smiled and asked me for a dance.

"You can lead, I'll follow"

"One day I hope you'll lead." She gave me a little wink and on the floor we went, smiling the whole night through so much that when I woke up the next morning my cheeks hurt.

She said to me as the night drew to a close, "On Wednesday you have to get your own lunch, I'm going to the music hall –in Detroit – for a dance matinee."

"What's that?"

"Dance theatre."

"The performers are going to be the Trocaderos Dance Troup"

I shrugged fine with it. She asked if I had ever been to the music hall. I said no. She said to me "Well, I have two season tickets for the music hall and the Fisher theatre maybe some time you can go with me." I said ok. Then she reached over, thanked me, and gave me a kiss goodnight and left.

I went on home and went to bed to get up the next morning to go back to work on the set. I was there at 9am sharp and people were already waiting there to help me on my first day on the job.

We had worked for about an hour when one of the members from the office told us Rose called and said she would be here around 11:30 with lunch. 'Holy cow' was the first thing I thought when she came in and told us all to go to the blue room and eat next to the kitchen. She had put out a spread of Hungarian lunch meats, chicken poppycosh, Hungarian potato salad, pop, water, coffee, and tea. There were only 8 people in the whole building and she brought enough food for a king and his whole court. I walked over to Rosemary with a happy surprised smile on my face.

"Wow, thank you, really, this is…awesome!" she gave an annoyed huff, rolled her eyes and lamely said,

"It's from mom to you…I think she has a crush on you" and I'm like, uh oh,

"Why?"

"Because you can fix things."

I just laughed and laughed while stuffing my face.

Afterwards, one of the workers stayed behind to help us clean up. He came up to me and nudged my arm.

"Soooo, what's up between you and Rosemary?" I just smiled and shrugged casually. "She's just my boss."

We went back to work and finished out the day. Rosemary came to check on me but I was exhausted mostly because the people who I was working with had no idea what they were doing and it was draining me trying to show them how to do things. I went home shortly after and passed out.

The next day, Rosemary brought in chicken noodle soup. It was "heavenly" because it had angel hair noodles in it. Rosemary's mother had made sandwiches with Hungarian bread and some kind of ham and cheese. I couldn't believe it – a Hungarian torte cake. All seven layers indeed. Rosemary started laughing,

"My mother is having waaay too much fun with this."

"Well," I hesitantly spoke. "She should stop, this is way too much." She grinned, "Nope, she's enjoying volunteering to help you out. She thinks you're the son she never had."

"Tell her I thank her very much and I owe her a kiss." Rose laughed and smiled at me and ended with,

"She'll collect."

The next day I showed up with the guys and we moved all the material upstairs to start building the set up to the brown room. We had worked and it was about 11:30 and we were getting ready to stop and go out to lunch and all of a sudden I hear this old lady's pretty voice hollering.

"Joseeeeeppphhh wheeeeere aaaaarreee yyouuuu?" She and Barney had three whole baskets filled to the brim with food. I was so embarrassed because I don't know the people around me! Barney and Margaret. went upstairs and put the food away and I told everyone to go upstairs into the blue room and have lunch. So they lined up and Barney said,

"Wait a minute. Joseph, I think Margaret is expecting something from you." I turned a deep, deep bright red. I walked up to her and said,

"Thank you MOM." and gave her a big kiss on the cheek. Barney just cracked up. Everybody ate and thanked them for their hospitality. After that I had double the helpers every time – just for the food. That night because I had leftovers I went straight home. Rosemary called shortly, thereafter.

"I hear you and my mother had quite an ordeal." I could hear Barney in the background saying,

"I have to have that young man leave my wife alone." They all laughed. I thanked Rosemary again for her family. I've never had so many people been so kind to me in my life. I asked Rosemary,

"What's the catch?" She honestly replied that this was her first show ever and her family was so grateful for me helping out. Also, that they realize that it wasn't paying much money and they felt bad. I told her in a playfully scolding voice.

"Rosemary, I'm not doing it for the money I'm doing it for the company." Her reply was sincere,

"Thank you... I'll see you tomorrow."

Finally after a week of long hours of nonstop laborious work – aside from lunch – it was Friday. Everybody else had something to do so I was working alone in the brown room on the floor making about 300 sets of legs for the staging when I heard the door open.

I saw a silhouette of a person walking towards but I paid no mind to it and kept working. He kept walking around inspecting all my work and listening to the radio. All of a sudden he reaches down and pinches me in the behind. I whirled around astonished and my eyes wide. I looked at the man and then down at the hammer in my hand but I realized I had no idea if it was a joke… or what!? I stood up with the hammer still in my hand and quickly walked, almost ran, out of the room and went straight to Rosemary's office.

I walked in and slammed the door shut feeling paranoid. Rosemary looked up at me and gave me a crossed look of worry and surprise.

"Rosemary! Do you know that man who just walked in?" I asked in a panicky tone. She's responded,

"Yaaaa, that's Jim why?" Well, I leaned in, looked over my shoulder to see if anyone was within earshot then I whispered,

"Well…I think he's *gay!*" Rosemary turned and narrowed her eyes at me then levelly questioned,

"… are you?" I looked her up and down and in an outraged voice said

"No!" She placed an almost mocking, cherry smile on her face and crooned,

"Then what are you worried about?"

In just less than a moment later Jim waltzed through the door with a puzzled look on his face. Rosemary waves Jim inside her office and tells him to take a seat.

"Jim, this is Joseph; he's building our set." He flashed me a toothy smile.

"I've seen it and I think he's doing a great job." Rosemary smiled. "Good. Now, Jim, Joseph is into ladies like me, not like you." Jim fakes a pout then winks at me and says,

"Oh well I couldn't help but try." We all laughed. By that time Rosemary had decided that we all needed to take a break. We sat around and she told me how she knew all these people from the theatre and Jim told me about all the plays he had been in. In the end, Jim became my friend and I realized he really was a great person.

The day ended with my face all red once again. When we had finished our meal Rosemary leaned over to Jim and goes,

"Watch this." He looked curiously as she slipped me the money under the table. He looked confused like 'what on earth?' but kept watching. Rosemary gave me a teasing smile and laughed then told him

"Joseph doesn't like girls paying for him so this is our little secret." I turned red.

Chapter 7

Final Details

So after a long weekend I set to work with a fresh crew. We all worked tirelessly through the week finishing up the set. Rosemary and her friends worked continuously on creating the costumes and gathering all the props. The air around me was always buzzing with excitement. It seemed like everyone was everywhere doing one thing or another, rehearsing, hammering, painting, and the like. I was never so astonished to see how much work it actually took to put together a production.

Rosemary was the mother hen of the nest. Whenever a fight broke out she was right there to put out the fire. She was the peacemaker. From that week alone I learned a lot about Rosemary. I remember, though, the biggest issue that she would always address was that the women and men always, *always* lied about their sizes saying that their waists were smaller or their chests were bigger, etc. To stop having to alter the costumes after discovering they didn't fit, she simply solved the problem by taking the tags off of everything and replacing them with name tags.

Since she always knew when they were lying, she simply measured all the performers herself.

It amazed me how everything slowly began to come together. Everyone's energy, everyone's pride, optimism, excitement, and expectations were running high. This alone made the work move faster. In fact, my crew finished the set early which gave more time to help out elsewhere. I was so proud how everyone pulled together in the end.

So by week's end the set was finished. Rosemary and I were in the blue room discussing how we should clean up so they could have their first rehearsal. We had been throwing compliments at each other the whole conversation. I kept going on and on about how amazed I was on how she did everything and she told me it was the same thing with me. She told me that we were visionaries. Me, in building, and her in costume creations. I stopped her before she could continue. I had never heard the term "visionary" before and hadn't had a clue of what it meant. She smiled at me and explained that it was a person who could see the concept in their minds before it became a solid reality. I smiled feeling important and special. Rosemary then smiled and looked at me,

"You know you really did earn your pay."

I laughed and said,

"You know...if I had known you sooner I would've done it for nothing."

Friday rolled along and I came and knocked out a few last minute hiccups and received my paycheck from Rosemary. Inside were two complimentary tickets for me and a friend to come see the show on opening night.

Chapter 8

Opening Night

As I remember it, Rosemary and I hadn't seen each other for the next two weeks. Her cast had been rehearsing nonstop for opening night and I was busy back with GM and my art. Though she was busy prepping for the show, Rosemary would occasionally call and keep me updated. From time to time I would stop by to come and fix anything that came up.

One time, I was called over because they had a plumbing problem, so I stopped by and repaired it. Everyone was surprised that I would just walk in and fix it for them because I had already finished my job. They didn't expect me to do charity for them. That was how I started touching up the building. Really, I was just happy to see my new friend, Rosemary.

As time crawled by we inched closer to opening day. Rosemary would often call me just to say hi. The last time she called she had asked me if I was going to use the other ticket and bring someone. I told her I didn't know if I was going to bring someone and if I did, I didn't know who yet. She immediately suggested that after the show, if I didn't bring anyone, we could go out to dinner. I told her okay, and we'd see. Ironically, about a half an hour later, my ex-wife, Gidget called me. She told me that she wanted me to pick up some leftover art supplies she had found that belonged to me. She started some small talk to keep me on the line, talking about her job and her insurance and her bills, etc. Then she finally got around to asking me what I'd been doing. I told her I had went back to work, got a new place to stay and restarted my life. I also had signed up to take adult education. We started talking about what I had been doing in my spare time and I told her I had just recently finished an odd job for a friend at the Wyandotte theatre where I built a set for their newest play. She didn't believe me so I offered her the extra ticket I had *from Rosemary* and to prove it she should come with me. She immediately asked me about Rosemary. After telling her a few things about Rosemary, I added that if she didn't want to come, Rosemary invited me out to dinner and the afterglow party anyway. Apparently, as soon as I had mentioned Rosemary's name, the idea of coming to the show with me suddenly seemed like a great idea. So instead of going to dinner with Rosemary, Gidget decided to cook dinner and insisted I stay and eat with her before we left.

I came over on opening night and we were extremely civil to each other (for a change). I put my stuff in my trunk and when I went back in she was finishing up dinner but told me there was something wrong with the sink. I fixed it then we sat down and ate. We talked and agreed that we were both sorry that it ended the way it did. Then we chatted about the families and just made small talk for the rest of the evening. Eventually it was time to go to the play. She went to the other room to freshen up. I distinctly remember that when she came out she looked very stunning. She came up to me, looped her arm in mine, and bashfully admitted she hadn't been to many plays before. So we got in my car and drove to the show.

As we pulled up she said it looked like an old abandoned building in a dump somewhere in the vast jungles of Detroit. In some ways, regrettably, she was right.

We walked to the front and climbed up the first set of stairs then went inside and climbed the next flight from the lobby. At the top was Rosemary with some of her theatre friends lounging around waiting for curtain call. As we walked by, Rosemary's eyes locked onto mine like steel. Instantly, I turned away feeling the moment tense up between me and the two women. I hurried Gidget along. (I didn't want to stick around long enough to see an event roll out between them.)

We walked to the ticket acceptance line and handed the lady our tickets and were seated in the front row. I knew that in the next few minutes the "mysterious lady with me" would be the talk of the century with all the theatre cast and crew, especially when everyone from the theatre that knew me was staring at me like I had grown two heads.

It was time for curtain call. The whole time I could feel Rosemary's eyes burning into me from stage left. I squirmed in my seat a little from time to time. As if Gidget could sense Rosemary's presence in the background, she discreetly made a show of putting her hand on mine and getting comfortable as she scooted closer to me. I felt my face begin to heat up.

Finally intermission rolled around and I almost leapt out of my chair in the urgency to escape the tension. Gidget and I went to get refreshments. The lady who served us to my dismay was Rosemary. I felt like I was in a nightmare. Rosemary set the drinks down at our table then turned to me and smiled very politely and said in a bittersweet, honey voice,

"Hello Joseph, who is this?" She offered me a smile – I knew it wasn't real because the smile didn't emanate from her eyes. I knew I was in a danger zone. Gidget spoke up then.

"Oh, you must be Rosemary" The gingersnap venom in her voice was left raw.

Rosemary did smile this time, but it was more of a curious smile with the slightest hint of a smirk dying to creep onto her lips.

"Joseph, won't you introduce us properly?"

"Uhh…ya... Gidget this is Rosemary; Rosemary, this is Gidget, my ex-wife." Rosemary nodded still smiling but this time Rosemary didn't bother to hide the distaste in her expression as she gazed at Gidget.

I took this as my cue to leave. I excused myself to the bathroom and had to use all the restraint I had not to bolt out of the room. When I came back Gidget was alone.

I walked over to her noticing she was deep in thought. I carefully looped my arm with hers and began the trip back to our seats. The whole time I could almost see the cogs and gears slowly grating against each other as they struggled to spin in Gidget's head. I could plainly see she was *not* happy. I realized that bringing her here was a tremendous mistake and began wishing that I had never brought up the theatre to her in the first place. I thought about saying something or asking her what happened but by the cold stare she was giving anything that came in her line of sight, I took the chance that I would live longer if I kept my mouth shut. We took our seats and watched the second part of the play. Gidget sat rigidly still and didn't say a single word the rest of the show. I was becoming tense and frustrated wondering *exactly what **did** Rosemary say to Gidget*. The play ended, we both stood up simultaneously, hands to ourselves, and headed straight to the door. The tension rolling off our shoulders was enough for people to steer clear of our way. Gidget did not stop to give me time to excuse us and say goodbye. She headed straight to the car. She waited for me to open the door not once making eye contact. I opened the door and she got in. I jogged to the other side and started the car.

"Joseph will you please take me home now?"

I said "Yes."

On the car ride home the silence was so thick you could slice it with a knife. We finally arrived after what felt like forever. The moment the car rolled to a stop, she opened the door herself and practically jumped out. She bent down with her purse tightly clung to her chest, she formally said thank you, shut the door and walked away. That was the last time I ever saw Gidget. *I never did find out what transpired while I was out of the room.*

Chapter 9

A New Start

The next day, first thing in the morning Gidget calls. She thanked me for coming over and fixing her sink. She had a nice time at dinner with me and it sort of reminded her of the good old days. *But*, she saw how I looked at Rosemary and told me it was obvious that she saw something between us. I laughed,

"Nah," I said, "Rosemary and I are just friends; we just click."

In the tone of voice she used afterwards it was clear she didn't believe me but she went along with it. We talked for a while but eventually she grew quiet and didn't have much more to say. She said goodbye and hung up. I finally recognized that what we had was now officially over.

That same day, Rosemary's mother called. She told me Rosemary came home last night and seemed distraught. She said Rosemary mentioned that I was with somebody by the name of Gidget. Her mother was curious as to what was going on. As I didn't want Rosemary upset, I began to explain to her,

"Gidget was my ex-wife and had called because she wanted me to pick up my stuff and fix her plumbing. While we were on the phone I told her about my job at the theatre and how she wouldn't believe me so I simply wanted to prove it to her. That's why I took her. I didn't mean to cause such a fuss. But, that last night Gidget understood there was no place for her in my life anymore. What was between me and Gidget is over. We're done."

Her mother politely hung up to go upstairs and talk to Rosemary. In a matter of minutes Rosemary was ringing my phone.

"What the *hell* was that?"

I explained everything all over again to her and kept apologizing in the process. I didn't mean to cause to such an uproar. I honestly just wanted to finally get the last of my stuff out of Gidget's house. I felt good that it was now completely over. It was as if a thousand pound weight was lifted off my chest. I finally felt free. The whole episode was an emotional roller coaster. All the counseling in the world couldn't help as much as what transpired that evening and that it was finally done. Rosemary sympathized and admitted she understood. I guess I just needed closure with Gidget so I could move on with the next chapter in my life. She then wondered aloud though what was to become of Buffy who was close with Gidget? I told her that now I have new friends and Buffy will have new friends too. She laughed.

"Are you gonna go to school with her?"

"If I have to, I will".

In retrospect I had no idea what I was doing or what was gonna happen. How on earth I was gonna pay bills, take care of Buffy, work, go back to school, and top it all off, stay an artist. But I knew I had a new life, new goals, and renewed hope. Somehow, I knew I was going to get it right this time.

CHAPTER 10

Rosemary, My Almost-Love

After that, Rosemary and I started talking everyday on the phone for hours and hours on end. She knew how I wanted to have my independence and find myself in the world and find my purpose.

Rosemary told me that she wanted to stick along for the ride and see what happens next. So, she invited me to the cast and crew party at the end of the run that was coming up that Saturday evening after the show.

I went, and to my surprise everyone knew who I was, what I did for the show, and that Rosemary fancied me more than just a little. I was so surprised by everyone I met that night and how kind they were to me. Generally thankful that someone came in and built the set for them, because they almost didn't have the show. I found out that I really enjoyed being the center of attention with all my new friends or friends in the making. I have to admit, I secretly felt elated when I noticed Rosemary's eyes following me around the room.

As the night was drawing to a close, the cast and crew started putting things away. I started to notice just how much food there was. I asked

Kissed by My Confidant

Rosemary who caters all this and she told me that her and her mother cooks the food and helps set up for the party. What I really noticed was how everything is done according to the period or better known as the "theme" of the show.

I was so impressed I had to try everything. Rosemary was fascinated by how much I enjoyed her and her mother's cooking. As you know they're Hungarian. I fell in love with the food, again.

Refusing to let the night end, Rosemary and I, along with a few friends went out to a local pub to go dancing and carry on the party. Between dances, Rosemary leaned over to me and said,

"Joseph, we still have some things to put away. I'll be at the theatre tomorrow after six why don't you come on down and we can chat while we finish things up.

The next day I showed up. I strolled into the brown room and started putting my stuff away. Rosemary was in the blue room cleaning up from the day before.

Some time had passed. I had broken down the set and was at the point where I needed help to move it in order to put it away. Other than that I was finished.

Right then, Rosemary happened to walk into the room with a smile on her face. With a glow she turned and waved me into the blue room. As I walked in my stride faltered and I just stood there with my mouth agape, gawking at the room. The entire span was just draped in candles. Candlelight danced across the floor with shadows flickering here and there across the expanse. In the middle of the room rested a low table with a white table cloth. For the centerpiece stood a candelabrum. There were cushions littering the floor around the table inviting me into a very comfortable seat. The heavy royal blue curtains hanging just below the high ceiling definitely accented the picture. The softest tune of Mozart was playing in the background. I was stunned.

Rosemary came out of the shadows with the biggest smile on her face I've ever seen. In that moment nobody has ever made me feel more special than she did right then and there.

"Joseph," she grins, "take a seat."

Almost without thinking I plopped down on one of the cushions and just couldn't stop gazing at her in awe. She looked almost like a young school girl, giddy with glee at my reaction. I was almost afraid to speak, because I feared if I did, all this would just disappear and fade like a dream interrupted.

Rosemary elegantly lowered herself down on to one of the cushions next to me. My stare followed her every movement. I felt like I couldn't get my brain to work. She couldn't stop smiling. Gazing into my eyes, she reached over and laid her hand over mine. At the contact I snapped out of my trance.

"Rosemary…what-what *is* all of this? There's nobody else here. What's going on?"

"This is for you Joseph. We both live with somebody and I didn't want to take you out to eat, I wanted to do something special to say thank you for everything that you've done."

"I- wait, what? This is for me?"

"Yep."

My expression said it all. Wow. She looked delighted.

"Joseph, I made dinner for the both of us. I'll be right back. When I get back I really want to get to know you. Okay?"

"Ok." She then excused herself and almost skipped away. When she came back, she didn't come empty handed. She came out with dish after dish of food. Chicken poppycosh, pork chops, German potato salad, cucumber salad, csiga noodles and chicken broth – which was just perfect, mixed vegetables, stuffed eggs, celery ala cream cheese, chocolate torte cake, and lastly, spumoni ice cream. I felt like a king. For the rest of the night we feasted and she drilled me with question after question. That evening, we shared our first real kiss. I was her savage beast and she was my beauty. That night, she vowed she was going to tame me.

The night was so special. I could not believe that this woman was into me this much. Doubt kept creeping into my mind. It kept whispering and hissing at me. My first two wives went from love to hate, will the cycle repeat itself with Rosemary? Despite my haunting thoughts, we stayed together talking until midnight.

During our conversation, I told her,

"I have to be truthful with you, I feel like I've missed something…I want to go out with others ladies but I don't wanna hurt anyone, especially you. I feel that up to now I had wasted my life on my past two wives and haven't really lived yet."

She leaned over gave me a kiss and said,

"As long as you don't lie or hide who you are from me, we'll work it out. But right now, your mine."

I looked at her and grinned,

"Ok. We can have fun, just don't get mad."

She put her arms around me and uttered,

"Deal."

Riiiiiing, Riiiiiing… I rolled out of bed and almost ended up on the floor. I looked at the time 8:00 a.m. on the dot. I shook my head trying to clear my drowsy state. Riiiiiing. I rubbed my eyes and as I got up I heard something crinkle in pocket. I snatched out a folded up little piece of paper. Riiiiiing. It said, *'Joseph, hope you haven't forgotten, my Moms making pork chops for us on Tuesday see you there!'* Riiiiinnnggg! I grabbed the phone and almost yelled into the receiver,

"WHAT!?"

"Hope you haven't forgotten me yet." Rosemary was on the other line laughing. I felt my face turn red.

"Oh, sorry!"

"I didn't wake you, did I? I told you I would call you in the morning."

"Oh, umm…no…its fine I was, um…I just…I thought it was just Phil's kids playing with the phone again," I shyly admitted. As Rosemary started talking, I started to zone out. I realized that she called me this early *just* to assess the results of the night before. She was serious about starting a relationship with me but I didn't want any part of it at that time, to be honest. Now, looking back, I realize I was afraid, afraid of getting hurt again. So, somehow I convinced myself, I wanted to be the untouchable bad boy. The kind of guy who liked women, had a little fun, but no more than that. I knew if I didn't put my foot down soon, I was going to get into a mess of things. But I also couldn't resist her mother's cooking. So when Rosemary asked me if I was coming on Tuesday, I couldn't help but say yes.

Chapter 11

My New Home

On Tuesday I showed up at Rosemary's place right on time. A wonderful pork chop dinner was waiting on the table. As with anything they cooked in that household, the chops were delicious. As we ate, we had several different side conversations going on simultaneously with different participants jumping in and out depending on the topic. They were digging for dirt on me right at the source. In one of those conversations Barney, Rosemary's dad, asked me what it was like to be single again. I couldn't help but note Rosemary pausing her conversation with her mother and leaning in, as she tends to do, to listen attentively to what I had to say.

"Well it hasn't really been perfect because now with everyone from the theatre coming over and sometimes my occasional dates; my family gets extremely uncomfortable with so many strangers in the house all the time, always coming in uninvited. Plus, they've started getting aggravated because the phone is always ringing," as I glance at Rosemary with a smirk;

"Rosemary is always taking me to these nice places and paying for them as is her preference and they are constantly arguing with me about whether that's appropriate or not. They keep trying to impose rules on me as if I was a young teenager: who I can go out with, when I should be home, and who can come and visit me, etc. It's become very stressful. Personally, I'm thinking about moving into my brother, John's house but he has a family of his own."

I didn't want to wear out my welcome so after the dishes were done I thanked everyone for the nice evening and headed home. The closer I got to home the more I thought about the conversation during dinner. By the time I arrived home, my mind was made up. The next day I moved into my brother's house.

---Well that didn't work out. I had spent little more than a month in my brother's house when I reached my limit. I couldn't handle it anymore. I had planned to do my artwork there and have a peaceful atmosphere. Deja vu happened. John and his wife acted just like Phil and his wife. I was very disappointed and frustrated. John's wife wanted me to do all the repairs in their house including completely renovating their kitchen while John wanted me to pay rent at the same time. Well, that was ok in the beginning but it got out of hand and became too much for me. I knew though instead of arguing about this, family was too important to let it be ruined over money. I had to move out.

While hanging out with Rosemary at Heidi's, as usual, I mentioned to her that I wanted needed my own space, I had to have a place of my own. That's when Rosemary decided to get involved.

Rosemary and her mother talked to some friends and began looking for a place for me to live that'd be closer to work. They called up people from everywhere. Her friends collected flyers and they investigated every single one of them to find the best apartment for me. Once they made their pick they called the man who was leasing it and made a deal with him. They said I was an excellent handy man and that if I didn't have to pay rent I would repair every single thing in the apartment building for free. The man agreed.

During their search, I had been working the line at GM every day. I was prepping for a new car paint job when the break whistle blew. I stopped working and was on lunch when I received a page from Rosemary (remember pagers?). When I called her back, she sounded thrilled over the phone and told me that I didn't have a choice; I was coming over to her house for dinner that night.

I went over that evening, kind of excited to find out what was going on. We sat down and Rosemary and Mom (as I used to call her mother) started sympathizing with me about how I was unhappy living with relatives and it was a tense situation for me and such. I, by now, had sort of lost my enthusiasm because this wasn't a happy subject for me then Mom turned to Rosemary and said,

"Rosemary, Sweetheart, go get that slip of paper and bring it to Joseph." Rosemary stepped into the other room for a second and returned to the dining room with the biggest grin on her face. My curiosity began to resurface.

"Joseph, Mom and I know that since you've been struggling with your family trying to live with them. We would like to help you. We've been combing through apartment ads and thought this one was the best one," she said as she handed me an envelope.

"We have an appointment to meet the landlord after dinner around 7."

I was confused to say the least. "What the heck is going on?"

"Well, we found you an apartment."

I was so stunned that I had near "strangers" treating me even better than family considering what Rosemary had just said. They continued on with their conversation as if they were discussing the weather and I wasn't even there. With both women on the couch and me in the middle, her mother told me straight out,

"Joseph, people don't like single men coming in and out of the house, all hours of the night. You have to be considerate of the family. This might escalate into a fight and if you might need your family down the road you might not have them so it's best that you accept that we have found the perfect apartment for you." I couldn't help but agree.

We finished our meal, did the dishes, and Mom rushed us out of the house.

"Don't you kids be late!" came Margaret's cheery voice as she slammed the door. As we pulled out of the driveway I could see Margaret waving out of the picture window. It was a sight to behold.

Rosemary started explaining to me that this apartment is really close to work and that'll make gas money cheaper, save time for me, and if my car breaks down I can still make it and besides, it's close enough that she can drive me around no problem. In the back of my mind, I'm thinking

'Oh no. oh noooo!' She's trying to own me. But I knew this was the best thing that could happen to me. It felt less like she was pushing herself into my life and trying to control it, but more like freeing me to live it.

As we pulled up in front of the apartment building, I noticed that I'd driven by this building in the past. We got out of the car and I raised my head to see beautiful marble steps leading up to the entry of the first floor. My heart accelerated. The building had a historical beauty to it. It was enchanting. It seemed to come from the art deco period. We climbed the steps and entered the main lobby. There was a sign that said 'managers office hit buzzer to enter'. We pressed the buzzer. A few moments later an elderly couple came down the hall, welcomed us, and offered us some tea.

"You must be Joseph; Rosemary has told me so much about you." We shook hands.

"Follow me, I'll show you where you'll be staying." We walked back down the hallway through the buzzer doors and stopped in front of a room labeled 'managers office'. I was baffled. As if reading my mind the man turned to me and said,

"Don't worry, my wife and I are only posing as the managers and maintenance of the building at the moment. Come on in and let me show you your apartment".

I was elated at the size, proximity, and layout of the space. The man turned to Rosemary,

"Oh, by the way, did you inform Joseph about our conversation where you told me that he is a good handyman and might be interested in doing some work for us?"

I turned and looked at her,

"Is that so? Well, what's in it for me?"

"Rosemary and I figured you would say that. Here's the deal. Rosemary is going to put down your deposit for you and one month rent. We will try you out for that one month and if everything works out your full rent will be cut in half, as long as you're our repairman; and we mean a *good* one too and eventually your rent will be completely cut out in exchange for you being the superintendent."

Lion Joseph P. Griggs

Joseph Apt. in Detriot

Joseph, the new super

"Rosemary, be a dear; please go sit with my wife while Joseph and I talk things over. Then he can take a look around and see what he would need to do."

Once we finished looking around the building we went back to his apartment with the women. His wife looked up at me and said,

"Well, what do you think?"

"I'll take it!" I smiled. A cheer went up around the room.

The man pulled out the paperwork. I filled everything out while his wife asked Rosemary for the deposit. Rosemary pulled out a thick brown envelope and started counting out hundred dollar bills. She handed over the money. Rosemary then rose, turned to me, held out her arm, and said,

"Now you have your own place."

Mrs. Rogers handed me two keys.

"You can start moving your stuff tomorrow; your first month rent is covered." She smiled and said, "I hope this works out for all of us." Rosemary plucked one key out of my hand and winked; she twirled around, smiled cheekily, and said back,

"Oh I *know* it will."

Mr. Rogers and I went out the door to have a cigarette to celebrate the finalization of the agreement. Rosemary came outside with the paperwork thanked him again, and excused us. She explained that we had to go because Mom and Dad were probably dying to know how everything went.

Chapter 12

Rosemary Becomes My Confidant

-A person with whom one shares a secret or private matter, trusting them not to repeat it.

As I climbed into the car I watched Rosemary pick her way daintily down the steps. As she slid into the car, she looked at me and said,

"Those nasty cigarettes are all over the ground, as the maintenance man you must pick them allll up. In fact, you better put out a can."

As we drove back Rosemary had a pleased look. She turned to me and asked,

"Do you feel like having a black Russian?"

"No, I want a rusty nail."

"Well, what are we waiting for? Let's go to Heidi's."

Now at our watering hole, we were drinking and nibbling on some tidbits, feeling content. Rosemary looked up and gently placed her hand on my arm.

"Have you realized that this is *our* booth? We always come to *this* restaurant and we always sit in *this exact* booth and we always have the *exact* same waitress. Would you like to know why?" I nodded curiously.

"It's because I love looking into your eyes. This spot has the best light to see you."

"Is that all?"

"No, I also love your voice." I smiled. She winked back and quickly became very serious.

"Joseph, I don't care what it takes. All I want to do is make you happy, take care of you, and have you there for me-" I cut her off guiltily,

"Rosemary, I'm sorry but you know you're not my girlfriend." Her shy but graceful, strong, demeanored smile never faltered.

"I know you don't like the word 'girlfriend' because of your history, so how about we pick another word? How about you call me your confidant?"

"Wow, I like the sound of that," And so she became.

"So, now that's out of the way, what do you like about me Joseph?" It was my turn to smile.

"I love your ankles (I'm an ankle man), I love your hair, and I love that smile."

"Is that all?" she pouted. Don't you like my eyes?" I feigned astonishment.

"Oh goodness, no, certainly I adore your voice, but not nearly as much as I always pay attention to your eyes. Even more, you're the only woman I've ever met that is a perfect lady all the time. It's so rare, and it's so beautiful. You are so rare, and you are so beautiful, My Confidant."

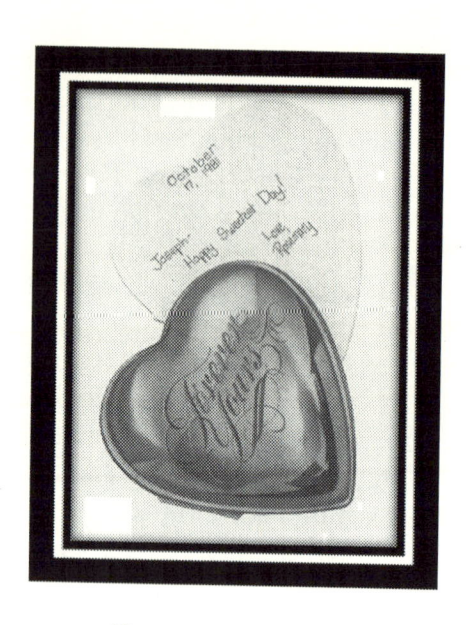

Chapter 13

The One-Sided Courtship

The next day, Rosemary called to tell me that she has tickets for the Fisher Theatre to see a dance recital and that she would be delighted to pick me up. She also pointed out that on our way we could move some of my things into my new apartment. Since it was a matinee, she mentioned that afterward we would go to brunch and see what we could do about furniture and whatever else we could find for the apartment. She also told me that she bought me season tickets to the Fisher and the Music Hall so that I could go with her so she wouldn't have to be alone. I told her thank you but she really didn't have to keep doing things like that.

In feeble attempts to try to get her to stop liking me, I would tell her that I was going out with this lady or that lady and she would always say

"Weeeelll lets make sure you look good!" and we would go out and she would pick out my clothes for the date. Or she would make shirts, ties, coats, and she would alter the clothes I already owned so they would look better on me according to her. She would call me at home and see what I was up to and make sure she would drop off things for me to make the dates more interesting. Often, she would insist on dropping me off on my dates, or pretty much anywhere because my ride was awful. We would go out to dinner and she would coax me into telling her how the dates went. The funny thing is when I would go out with the other ladies, they would ask me about places I've been and I would tell them about going to the Fisher and the Music Hall and they would ask me how I was able to purchase all those tickets. I would tell them *My Confidant,* Rosemary, has two season tickets, one for her and one for me so I could escort her to the shows. But what would always happen with all the girls I went out with was, somehow, they'd meet Rosemary or hear too much about her and then disappear.

One time, I was on my way to Wayne County Community College since I was starting my profession as an artist and interior designer. I had a class working in anatomy and they would bring in the models - to my surprise, they were nude. I got embarrassed and everyone in the class started laughing because I had turned red. I walked out. That evening, I told Rosemary what happened and she said I should see if I can make up the assignment. I went back to the instructor and he said that if I contacted the model and she agreed to allow me to redo the drawings he would allow me to enter them for a lower grade because I had walked out of the class. I agreed and made the phone call, but she never called me back.

Two weeks later, I was working on the apartment and Rosemary called me to go to the matinee. I asked her to grab our friend, Dave to fill in for me for me since I was stuck finishing up my homework and some plumbing. That morning, while I was finishing up the plumbing, one of my neighbors in the building came to me and said that there was a lady out front looking for you and she's waiting outside your office. To my surprise it was the model from school. She said she had gotten my message, was in the neighborhood, asked me to redo the assignment right then. I was a bit taken by surprise but said 'sure.' She walked into my apartment and asked me if I understood that she normally didn't do nude poses for private artists outside of class but the instructor informed her that it would save my grade. So reluctantly, she had agreed.

As I gave the model the nickel tour of the apartment, she mentioned that she thought my bed was beautiful and asked if that was where she could pose.

Lion Joseph P. Griggs

Joseph and his Japanese wedding bed

    I stammered and rambled out the story of that bed. The month before during the holidays, Rosemary and I were going through JC Penny's department store talking about getting a new bed for me. The store was displaying a Japanese wedding bed. It was amazing. Rosemary bought it for me as a Christmas present and had it delivered. I adored that bed. Everybody loved that bed. *Everybody,* including the model. When she laid eyes on my bed, she insisted we do it there since it was so comfortable and would make a great setting for the artwork. So, I moved the easel in while she laid out some satin sheets that I had then disrobed and posed on them.

    I was finishing up the painting when I heard the key turn. There was Rosemary and Dave back from the show. I didn't even have time to stand. Dave howled,

    "Excuse me!" as he darted out of the room; he was so embarrassed. Then there was silence and it was tense. Rosemary walked over to the easel and said,

    "Joseph, aren't you going to introduce me?" I gave her the lady's name, and Rosemary introduced herself then turned to me and said.

"Joseph? Was this the homework you told me about?" I said no but it *is* homework. I had no idea that the model was coming by to complete the makeup homework.

"Well, Joseph, you don't look red now." I threw up my hands and stormed out leaving the two women alone in the room. Rosemary and the lady spoke for a bit and when I returned she was dressed and they both walked out of the room together. Rosemary didn't say a word to me.

"Dave! We're leaving now!" For a fleeting moment I actually thought that whatever Rose and I had was over.

I hadn't heard from her for a week. And then, one day like nothing happened I got a phone call from her. I told her I had received a B on my "homework." I eventually ended up with a B+ for my semester grade. From that point on, I had no more women coming to that apartment. I owed Rosemary that at least.

Our friendship steadily grew stronger over the next year and a half as we became more involved with community theatre. During that time I became the manager of the building but the neighborhood was getting rough. One day when we came home, someone had totaled my car in front of the building. Rosemary told me that maybe it was time to move back downriver (closer to her). I told her I would think about it.

I switched duties at GM and became a team leader who filled in as a relief man. In my down time I started doing artwork at Cadillac and my bosses didn't mind as long as it didn't interfere with my work. In fact they even bought some of paintings. My life was finally coming together.

I don't know how or why but for some reason Rosemary and I just got closer and closer. She loved my daughter, Buffy. They acted just like best friends. But I thought I should still be seeing other women. I was no longer sure about what I was going to do next.

This era was the beginning of the most fun I've ever had in my life. Rosemary and I would go out in the evenings to avoid the sun, sometimes going to the theater and sometimes going dancing, and if she couldn't dance she had her girlfriends come and dance with me. Some nights, we didn't get home until three or four in the morning. We went to every show that came to town. She was a member of the musical theatre, the art museum, the Southgate Players, the Wyandotte Players, and the Huron Players. We went to modern dance at the Music Hall. We would even go out of town for some other shows. I had to admit, it was nice to go out with a woman who knew how to dress, talk, and act always as a lady. She had the clothes, the education, and the background of an aristocrat but at the same time she would go into some of the poorest communities and educate the people to get their GEDs. She never looked down, she never looked up; she thought everyone was equal, just a different ambience in life.

There was a time when she knew I was dating other women that I almost didn't want to be around her. It bothered me because I believed she would accept me no matter what phase of life I was in as long as I was in her presence even without any true commitment. She always told me that the only difference from one person to the next is their willingness to accept what they can or what they cannot do and be willing to accept others the same way. She always said where one person leaves off the other person picks up so everyone has different callings and some callings are talent, education, life experiences, and such but when you add them up, that's what makes a whole person and what they are willing to do in their lives, which is what led me to my decision.

Chapter 14

The Proposal

After many months of Rosemary courting me, I was getting tired of every woman I met wanting more of a commitment than I wanted to give. None of them were just right. I had just been awarded a fantastic dinner at the Top of the Flame Restaurant in Detroit, and it was for two, but it was for the daughter of one of my art clients. The lady and I knew each other from work as an artist. It was no secret that she fancied me. I agreed to go to the dinner since it was an extra thank you for my work. There was something strange about that night, though. I really would've liked to have taken Rosemary, but this was their gift to me so I had to go along with it.

We sat down and we started talking about music and such. When she heard I was an artist that was into theatre and went to a different show almost every week, the first thing she asked was how on earth I could afford to go to all of these events. I then told her about Rosemary. She asked me how I could afford all the clothes. I told her they were all gifts from Rosemary. The conversation continued on as we ate until it was time to go to the show. The more questions she asked the more I seemed to talk about Rosemary. After the show we went for dessert.

As we sat there speaking she noticed I was in another place, far in my mind. About two thirds of the way into dessert, she interrupted the conversation. She seemed a bit sad but she told me honestly that my topics always turned to Rosemary and that I was clearly out with the wrong woman. She ended the date early by saying,

"You know, Joseph, I would love to find a man like you for myself, even if you can't see it, you are obviously in love with Rosemary. You should really go home to her, where you belong." The she stood up, gave me a kind smile, thanked me for the company and left. I didn't know it then but it would be the last date I would have with anybody besides Rosemary for the next quarter century. I sat there baffled. Letting everything click.

Any girl that I dated was always missing something. Looking back, I didn't like any of them because I kept comparing them to Rosemary. I already had everything I wanted and I just didn't see it. Understanding that all this time I had been looking for the person who had been with me all along, I felt so guilty. *What do I do?*

I do most of my best thinking on my drives home and this time the more I thought about everything, the more I knew things would never be the same. For the first time, I found myself being jealous of myself. This was what every man could have ever wanted and for years I had that, and I tried pushing it away. I had no idea what I had.

The next week, Rosemary and I had a party to go to. It was a wedding of a friend. All the guys had had too much to drink including me so Rosemary drove me home. I stumbled out of her car and some other drunken bastard walking along stopped to flirt with Rosemary. I had some choice words for him, he cursed something back at me, and we got into a fistfight. I was so drunk I couldn't defend myself and he kicked my butt and left me lying on the sidewalk. Rosemary ran out crying, helped me up, and half dragged me into my apartment. She dressed my wounds, put me in bed, and told me she would call me in the morning to check on me.

I woke up about two in the morning feeling really stupid. I called Rosemary around an hour later and apologized to her.

"I feel like a fool. I'm wasting my life playing these games. I should've kept my mouth shut. I was in no shape to get into an argument like that."

She calmed me down and cheered me up. We talked for about an hour. Then, I cracked.

"You know, I've been calling you my confidant for all this time, when, really, I knew that you loved me. Now, I want you to know that I love you. I think it's time that we take the next step. What do you think about us getting married?" There was a moment of silence on the other line as well as a sob of laughter.

"Well you know, I asked you first." That was her way of saying yes.

Chapter 15

The Rumor Mill

As soon as she got off the phone with me, Rosemary went screaming to her mother. They became ecstatic. They went and told her dad and he refused to believe it. Her mother called my mom. My mom called my family. Her mom called my family. Rosemary called her friend who called friends from the theatre and from the schoolhouse. They called people and it just went around like wildfire. The next morning when we got to church everyone knew about it. That gave us a chance to talk to the priest about what us getting married would entail before I talked to her parents about it.

I still had to ask her father for her hand. He *really* made it hard because he didn't want Rosemary hurt. I had the reputation of being a player. With her condition, if anything happened, it could really set her back and hurt her. He had some conditions I had to accept if I was to be able to marry her. He was worried that Rosemary and I living alone could be a problem with her health because I certainly didn't have the money to pay for her medical bills and I didn't have years of experience to know what to do with her. I also had to become Catholic before I could marry her. Plus I would have to take her to church every Sunday I could. Her father also said we had to wait a full year before getting married. 1 year - 12 months - 365 days – 8760 hours – 525,600 minutes, - 31,536,000 seconds. Rosemary was already counting down. I replied to him that I carefully weighed every condition individually. I explained that I understood I'd have to work extra hard to care for her medical condition and that I could get insurance through GM. I added that I did consider the conditions as important as well as fair. I loved Rosemary so much that I find them easily surmountable.

The day after we received her parents blessing I got to my office and at 6:00 am I had over a hundred calls waiting for me in my message box. Within 48 hours even my ex-wife knew. Old friends that I had nearly forgotten were calling me and old friends of hers were calling her, half to congratulate her and the other half because they didn't believe it. Our friends and family threw us a really nice engagement party. It was funny to listen to all the advice from everyone. Everyone had an opinion. Some truly believed in us while others warned each of us about the dangers that threatened our happiness such as her health and my past record of instability. Everyone else was happy but inside I was scared. I realized this time it was going to be different. I knew I was going to have to work hard to make this one succeed. But I concentrated on the fact that I had the support of her family and they believed in me where no one really had before.

Rosemary had a smile on her face that would not quit. She was enjoying every moment of her wedding planning. Now, since I moved closer to her (after my car had been totaled in front of my apartment), she was over almost every day. I started looking forward to it myself, counting down until the time of her usual visit.

One day, Rosemary called; thrilled to tell me she found a house for us in Lincoln Park. We had looked at about 10 houses but this one blew the others away. The price was perfect and with a little handyman work it would be perfect. It was built around the turn of the century (circa1900).

Rosemary and I went to meet the real estate agent. To my surprise the house had been unlived in and presumed haunted for around the past 5 years. It was spooky when we entered the house plus it stunk horrendously. Everything was dusty but the house was still completely furnished. Clothes, dishes, tools, appliances, everything was still there. It looked like whoever lived there just left vanished leaving everything remaining just as they left it. When I asked what happened, the agent said that this house was considered haunted. The last person who lived in this house was thought to have died in what I now call the library. He died of a heart attack. His family was part of the founding fathers of Lincoln Park, yet they were indifferent about his belongings and just left everything in the house.

Rosemary turned to me and asked me what I thought about it. I turned to the real estate agent and said we would think about it. The agent looked at me funny. I looked at Rosemary.

"Surprise! I already bought it; it's cheap and with a little fixing up, it will be perfect." I looked at her shaking my head. I had just gotten my loft and it was huge but it was up 2 flights of stairs. Rosemary wouldn't be able to climb those steps every day. I also knew she was right.

1906

1925

1982

My financial situation was disastrous and this house was affordable even by my standards. I sighed and turned towards her,

"This is A LOT to fix up, even if it's fixable, are you sure?"

"Yes, Joseph."

"Alright, then."

I also remember her parents coming over and her father's shocked comment,

"Oh My God, this is going to be a lot of work." – I am still working on it today August 2014. Her mother joked asking if someone died in the house. She had no idea how right she was.

Well, Rosemary and I started working on the house and planning the wedding at the same time. My friend, Rick, would be the best man and her sister, Suzan would be the maid of honor. It was going to be a simple wedding. But first the priest wanted us to go through marriage counseling because I had already been married twice. When we started the classes, I began to get angry. They were talking about things for people who were getting married for the first time. I already knew the drill and I felt that this was aggravating.

One day, I called Rosemary but she didn't answer. I called her 3 or 4 times. She hadn't arrived in picking me up for my class nor was she answering the phone. I was so nervous that I drove over to her place in my old junky car and used the spare key to get into her home. I had a horrible feeling. I opened the door and there she was lying on the floor. Her mother didn't realize what had happened. Rosemary appeared lethargic. We immediately took her to the hospital. They ran some tests.

Lion Joseph P. Griggs

Meanwhile Rosemary recovered but we had no idea what had happened. Shortly after her release, her doctor called and asked her to come back into the office the next week. During the office visit the doctor informed her that the findings showed she had developed Myasthenia Gravis or MG, an autoimmune neuromuscular disease which causes fluctuating muscle weakness and fatigue but there is medication for it. Rosemary started crying, knowing that it was just one more burden on her back. She told me she thought we shouldn't get married anymore. I grabbed her wrists and demanded she look me in the eye, I assured her that we would see it to the end, that anything could happen to me too, and that the house was cheap enough that we could still live in it if things got worse and we could continue on. She wiped her tears, drew herself up, and with a quivering lip she nodded. And we did.

Our friends started coming over to help us speed up the process of getting the house ready for the wedding. The house was in really bad shape. So we decided to do 2 or 3 of the main rooms and just paint and clean up and remove all the stuff that was no good. We ended up having a garage sale that lasted almost 4 weeks and by God that gave us just enough money to pay for the wedding.

CHAPTER 16

One Year Countdown

During this time I was still working at the Fleetwood, Cadillac plant while Rosemary was going back to teaching full time having just finished her master's degree. Everything seemed to be moving in the right direction until her father had started having some heart problems. This unexpected turn caused us to re-evaluate whether or not we should postpone the wedding. Her father's health was a negative factor and so was Rosemary's but the sooner we were married, the sooner Rosemary could fall under my insurance, a major over riding, positive factor; so in the end we decided to stay the with the original date. This also made Rosemary glad because it kept her on track with the one year countdown.

The usual disagreements arose between the two mothers-in-law to be. We were trying to set up the exact date to try to satisfy between what my mom wanted, what we wanted, and what her family wanted. God knows I've been through this before. It's tough finding a date that makes everyone happy juggling people's work, commitments, and health issues. My best man, Rick Z, was in Ohio in the seminary. His brother had been living with me (Martin the bartender). Rosemary's sister resided in Chicago. Practically no one in the wedding lived in the state of Michigan so we finally put our foot down and set the date and decreed we weren't going to change it. Period. October 1st, 1983 – and we kept it.

My daughter Buffy, 11 years old at the time, wasn't for or against the wedding; either way, she just wanted to see me happy. She loved Rosemary and her family and she loved my family too. It was, however, the differences after the divorce between her mother and me that made things difficult. At this time Buffy was my whole life. I never wanted it to change.

On top of concentrating on my art, maintaining my job at GM, moonlighting as a cook, fixing up the house, and juggling with all the wedding "crap", my mother would constantly tell me how difficult I was being concerning the wedding preparations because I wouldn't let her change the wedding plans to match what she thought was best. I knew she meant well but it was stressful getting her to compromise since it *was* Rosemary's wedding. Her first wedding as opposed to my third.

To reduce stress, my friends and I started having a poker night at my place once a week so I could decompress. Saturdays became late night penny poker. And my friends would egg me on knowing that I was very fussy with the whole situational wedding plans but they also helped me with the house so it was worth it.

One Saturday just before the usual game, Rosemary stopped by to tell me that we were signed up for marriage classes at the St. Henry's Catholic Church.

I had to work really hard to convince the church to accept the reasons why my past marriages didn't work and to satisfy the requirements of the Catholic Church. After some time, Rosemary and I had demonstrated to the church and our families that this was what we both really wanted and wished for. The church said it would take a more than a year for the paperwork to move through the Vatican. Rosemary refused to delay our life together. She convinced the church to give us the approval to get married. However, it couldn't be in a Catholic Church. They said that we would need to return to have the Church bless the nuptials after the paperwork came in from the Vatican. My father-in-law to be accepted this approved compromise which was equally as important to us. Now we could move forward.

Chapter 17

Final Wedding Preparations

Amidst the wedding plans and renovating the house, I found out I was being transferred to Poletown (the Detroit-Hamtramck Cadillac plant). Just when things were improving it started to get hectic all over again. Besides my transfer, Rosemary also was transferred to a new school because of cutbacks in the district, in addition to the family's illnesses, time with my daughter getting squeezed, and little time left for my artwork (which as you know by now always upsets me). Lastly Rosemary was starting to have a really hard time with her hands and will need an operation right after the wedding.

Meanwhile Rosemary and her friends were starting to sew, pick out the color scheme, and plan the menu. She was falling more in love with me every single day. With all her dedicated sewing, we had a whole theatre full of clothes. She and all her friends had a ball playing dress up. Everyone knew Rosemary adored vintage and Victorian era clothing and she enjoyed dressing me up in the same period.

Lion Joseph P. Griggs

Around this time, being with the theatre, we were invited to a charity auction featuring de-accessioned articles from Greenfield Village/Henry Ford Museum in Dearborn. We attended the function with some friends and found a jewelry counter of vintage rings. I was looking at the diamonds. My jaw dropped when I realized I couldn't even afford the minimum bid. As we looked around, Rosemary kept going back to this one little box until I saw tears in her eyes. Then she cried out,

"That's it!" There was an 18th century garnet ring in rose gold.

The rings

World War II era wedding dress

That's when Rosemary's friend came up with an idea. She had an aunt that had an old wedding dress from World War II, but it had never been worn because her fiancé died in the war. Her friend's aunt was so happy at Rosemary's reaction when Rosemary saw it. The ladies had her try it on and astonishingly it fit her like it was made for her. It was like fate. The ladies were so giddy that when they called me to tell me about it, I jokingly thought to myself, 'Well, there's no way out now.'

The next week, phone rang yet again. This time it was Rosemary's sister, Susan whom at the time worked at Tiffany's. She had gotten a great deal on a wedding ring for me. She came in from Chicago to show us the ring. The second I said I liked it she snatched it back, sized my finger, and had Rosemary whisper in her ear how she wanted it inscribed. I didn't get to read the inscription until I was married. What? You want to know what it said? It's personal.

Okay, I'll tell you. Inside the ring read *Love you always, Rosemary.*

After the ring, Rosemary took me to the brand new Sax Fifth Avenue in Fairlane Mall. We opened an account, picked out my entire outfit for the wedding right down to my shoes and had my suit fitted. I felt pretty snazzy to say the least. It seemed as if for the moment everything was perfectly falling into place.

I still had to have the house prepared enough for the reception. We had about 8 months to get it done because of the now rock solid deadline of October 1st 1983. To my surprise when Rosemary and I started planning the wedding, the one thing we wanted to do most, was to do all the food ourselves. Both families went nuts over this. They argued that we shouldn't have to cook for our own wedding. Despite the fact that both families differed on most things, this was one thing they definitely agreed on. They badgered and tormented us until Rosemary and I both finally gave in.

The outer family came together and all agreed on bringing a wide variety of catering foods. Rosemary's mother, however, insisted on making a Hungarian torte cake for the wedding. It was seven layers and each layer had seven layers to it. I had to restrain myself from tackling her mother in a great big bear hug. If it was Rosemary's mother making the cake I knew that from the first bite, I would think that I had died and went to heaven, then come back for another slice.

When we got down to 3 weeks before the wedding I had my bachelor party at the house.

Lion Joseph P. Griggs

Thumbs up to the bachelor party

There were about 25 of us in all, between Fleetwood, theatre, good friends, family and school. We had food, 2 cakes, LOUD music, horseplay, poker, and other guy stuff. It was golden – until my friend, Hal went upstairs to use the bathroom. We heard this big crash and he came running down, screaming

"Did u see that?!?! We just stared at him wondering what he was talking about. His face was all white. Three of us went upstairs and found a 4ft x 2ft mirror smashed on the floor. That wasn't the weird part. It wasn't even in the room where it was hung. I asked Hal if he moved it and he vehemently denied being anywhere near it. He told us that while he was in the bathroom he heard a crash. Then, while coming from the bathroom, he heard something down the hall and saw someone in front of him. He thought we were playing a prank on him. Then, another guy spoke up saying earlier he thought he heard a baby crying but didn't want to say anything. No one had been living in the house for 6 years. But they knew the tragic endings of those who had died while in the house. As the hair began to stand up on the back of everyone's neck, the men transferred the party into the garage. The guys were getting superstitious. Everyone had been drinking and with the ghost's visit, all the guys were on edge and the party started to elevate. Well, it wasn't long after that when the police showed up with a complaint about my party from the fire department across the street. They had had it with all the noise, the arguing, and even a fistfight they witnessed over who had helped me with the wedding but their main complaint was that our music was louder than their sirens. I guess it was kind of funny since we had thought we picked the perfect spot for our party because except for the fire department we were practically in the middle of nowhere. So the radios were turned off, the food and drinks were put away and one by one, my friends trudged out of the garage to go home. But I had 3 brave friends that slept over. And that's when the real trouble started. All night there were odd noises and sounds of movement in the house. In the morning, the men wanted to go home bad and didn't want to work on the house anymore. They claimed it was haunted. I freaked out and told Rosemary the next day because there was no way I could get the whole house ready in time for the reception all by myself.

Rosemary went to the school where she taught and talked to some friends who said they knew someone who could perform a séance and would find out what the problem was and take care of it.

I wasn't there during the séance because I had to work. All I know was from what Rosemary told me the next day. Rosemary had a medium come by who went through the house doing some spiritual stuff and told me no more worries that they had made peace. Supposedly, the spirits were concerned that something was going to happen to the house. She communicated to them that we were there to take care of "their home." I'll never know exactly what happened but I know that the noises and freaky things in the house stopped. So my friends came back and we rushed through and had it ready just in time for the wedding.

Lion Joseph P. Griggs

Painting the garage for the wedding

I will never forget the look on Rosemary's face when she came in for the final inspection. She was so happy because with all her health issues, she didn't think she would ever get married.

Now it was two days before the wedding, people had been calling the house all day long. My father and I had recently finished the library by refinishing some antique bookcases and all I had to do was put the books away. I was on a ladder putting a giant Shakespeare book on the top shelf when the phone rang, I reached down to answer and the book fell on my face and cut my cornea. I could hear my mother on the other end of the phone. I hollered out to her what happened as I was cupping my eye. She rushed over and took me to the hospital but they didn't have a specialist to take care of a paper cut to the eye. They had to send me to a specialist in Trenton about 20 minutes away. When we went to the specialist, he determined that to fix it then would have knocked me out of the wedding. The best he could do to keep me in the game was to freeze my eye and do a temporary patch job. He told me that my eye would be black (largely dilated) for a while but would heal enough to get me through the wedding. Until then, whenever it hurt (which was all the time), I had to use eye drops, take pain medication, and wear an eye patch. For my wedding I ended up having one black eye that made me look like the devil and the other sky blue. What a contrast. When Rosemary saw me all she did was roll her eyes and said,

"It could only happen to you."

Through all the wedding planning chaos, Rosemary was still teaching theatre and working on the costumes for a play. It was just awful trying to do all that in such a small window of time. But with so much to do, the time flew by and before we knew it, the countdown was complete and the wedding day had arrived.

CHAPTER 18

Third Times A Charm (Wedding Day)

While I was playing doctor to my eye, Rosemary and her family were going nuts the morning of the wedding. I was NOT allowed to see Rosemary at all before the wedding. The maid of honor and her date arrived from Chicago and let us use his Continental as the wedding car.

Rick drove me to the church. My family showed up, begrudgingly, being my 3rd wedding. I just wanted to get the damn thing over. Her mother stopped into the Groom's ready room at the church to wish me well and told me Rosemary was glowing. She said if I had ever made anyone happy in my life it was Rosemary. Rosemary's mother dabbed her eyes as tears of joy trickled down. She told me Rosemary was one of those people who believed in romance and love and the fairytale, and up until then it always seemed like she would never be able to have that in her life. Now, I was making a princess's dream finally come true. Then she gave me a mother's kiss and said she had to go because it almost time for the wedding to begin.

Kissed by My Confidant

Rosemary reflecting on her future

After one final check in the mirror Rosemary was ready for what was to be the happiest day of her life.

Just before it was time for Rick and I to take our places, my mom and dad popped in and asked if they could take a picture of just the three of us.

My parents and I

Lion Joseph P. Griggs

The time for well wishers, final touches, practicing our lines was behind us. Just like in the theatre, rehearsals were over. The audience had taken their seats and it was the moment for the curtain to go up. It was time. As we stood at the end of the aisle watching, the music began playing and everybody stood.

First came the Maid of Honor.

Maid of Honor and Best Man

Then there she was. Her hair was up in her classic bun, with a wreath made of baby's breath decorating it. Roses, carnations and candles adorned the church. I remember as her father walked her down the aisle, she hid her deformed her hands with her bouquet from the people who didn't know her. She was absolutely stunning in every detail. Rosemary's expression that day was almost indescribable, she had a victorious look about her as if everything she had been put through was worth it and had finally paid off. She was no longer a princess, she was a queen. There are not enough words to describe how she looked. I could barely breathe.

Kissed by My Confidant

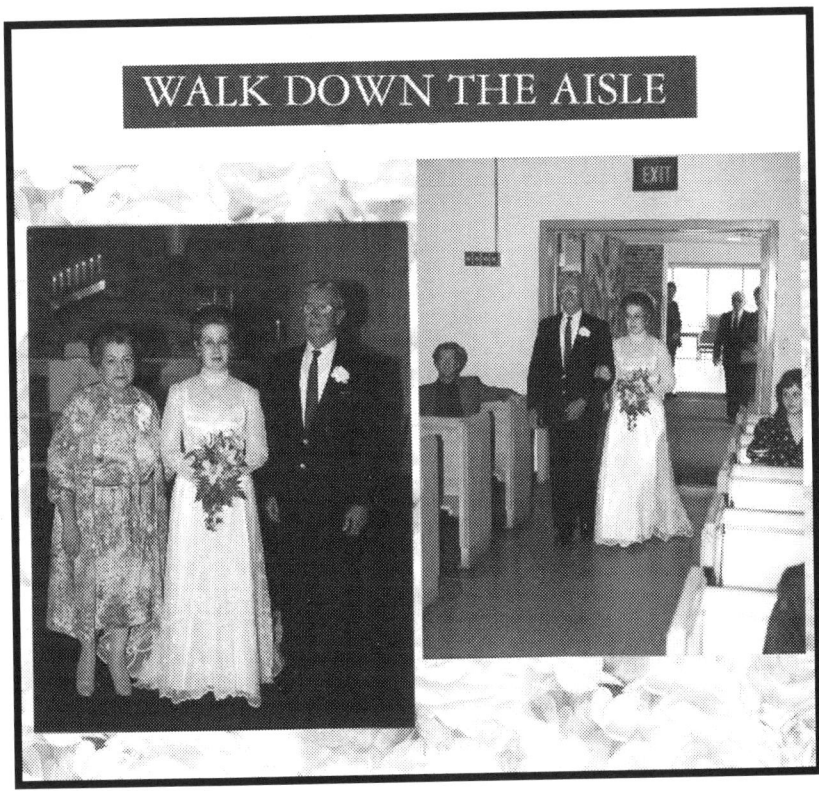

WALK DOWN THE AISLE

Rosemary and her parents

By the time we had finished exchanging our vows, I knew that Rosemary had always been the one I was searching for. I knew she would stick by me forever and she would forgive me for putting her through so much just to get to this spot in our lives. After 2 failed marriages in a year and a half and 5 years with Rosemary, there she stood as my wife squeezing my hand so tight I thought it was going to break off.

Lion Joseph P. Griggs

With friends and family from both sides, the wedding was still small with maybe about a 100 people.

Kissed by My Confidant

I was so happy Buffy was there to see it all.

Then we went from the church to our house for the reception. Every chance she could, all night long, she kissed me. We had set up 2 bars, one in the basement and one in the garage. There was food in the garage, basement, kitchen, dining room, parlor, library, and the front porch. The amount of food was ridiculous. Friends were eating and drinking all through the house with no ghostly interruptions. We had someone playing a piano and all our friends from the theatre were singing and telling stories of all the shows we had worked on together. We had Rosemary's friends from her school. We had friends from my art classes. My friends from when I worked as a cook and a chef for the Calipori Brothers, and my best friends from the paint shop at the Fleetwood plant. People stayed past midnight even though the party started at 5 in the afternoon.

Lion Joseph P. Griggs

At the end of the reception about 10 of our closest friends were sitting in the parlor when the clock struck midnight. One of my friends looked at me and said

"Joseph, where are you two going for your honeymoon? We thought you would have left already." I told him,

"Well, to tell you the truth we're staying here. We are both going back to work on Monday and in a few weeks; Rosemary has to have surgery on her hand. We are using the money to make sure we can handle the cost of the operation. We are going to go on our honeymoon at a later date." We started fantasizing about the future honeymoon. We were bouncing around ideas like going to Hawaii, Australia, Hungary, or Niagara Falls. Though, there was this desire we had when we were dating. We both knew that I always wanted to go to Paris and be a street artist. We also both knew that Rosemary had an elegant ruby red evening dress with a slit down the side that she would wear just for me during special events at the Fisher Theatre and the Music Hall. Our dream was to actually go to Paris where I would be working with my paints on the street while Rosemary was at the hotel putting on my favorite dress and getting dolled up. With Rosemary in the red dress, she was to come down the street pretending to be a street walker and tap me on the shoulder. I'd turn around and we'd fall into each other's arms then stop into a local pub where we'd have the juke box play a really pretty, slow song, *The Lady in Red* by Chris De Burg and dance just the two of us. Then we'd laugh the night away as we walk into one restaurant after another trying all the different foods, enjoying each other's company, seeing the sights, and kissing all through the night. That was our fantasy honeymoon.

Chapter 19

Tick-Tock, Tick-Tock As Time Goes By

The one thing we did not want to do for our honeymoon was to go down south and visit my family or go and visit hers. We had enough of family for a little while. We laughed about it but what we truly wanted was her health. We hoped that the operation on her hand would be the last she would need. But it was only the beginning.

Consequently, shortly after we married Rosemary had all the joints in her fingers replaced with a new experimental material. She had this done a decade before but it didn't last. I was in the waiting room pacing until the operation was over. When they finally brought her back to her room, I just sat at her bedside waiting for Rosemary to wake up. It seemed like forever until a doctor finally walked in and told me that it wouldn't be until the afternoon before she would regain consciousness. So, I went to work.

Kissed by My Confidant

After work I came straight back to the hospital to see Rosemary. When I walked into the room, she was awake. She smiled at me and beckoned me to come over. I bent over her to say hello and she slapped me. She told me **never to leave her alone again** because she will always expect me to be there when she wakes up since I was now her husband.

After she recovered, Rosemary went back to teaching, over the following six months or so, she began to have complications with her new medication which resulted in atrocious side effects and as a result she was gradually getting physically weaker and weaker.

During this stage, Rosemary was having a hard time commuting to school, so she decided to buy herself a new car. By having a car that was now easier to get in and out of and easier to drive, it helped her sustain at least a few more years of teaching. It was a Chevy Tracker, and at first she had a hard time getting used to it. In fact, one day, we were standing in the driveway talking and she looked at the car said she would like me to turn her around. She had actually meant turn the car around but I took it literally. I gently grabbed her by both shoulders and turned her around. She didn't think it was very funny at the time scolding me for being a trickster when she was in a hurry. Later on though, she laughed.

A year later they she had a knee replacement. Two years later they replaced the other and then she had 2 foot operations. The rheumatoid arthritis was forcing Rosemary to start seeing more specialists. Within two more years both hips needed to be replaced. She worked only one more semester after the hip replacements which was devastating to her. She was determined to get back to work.

Her hearing and sight began to deteriorate due to her medication. The myasthenia gravis prevented her from remaining standing over long periods of time, so we had to have a wheelchair made for her. In order to transport Rosemary in her wheelchair we bought a special van with a lift. I was NOT happy since I am strictly GM and it was a Ford. Rosemary was able to teach school for another semester. She was so pleased because she thought she was making progress.

Around Thanksgiving we went to see a specialist about her arthritis. The doctor ran a bunch of new tests and we ended up being there for the whole day. During lunch Rosemary was telling me about how she felt that her hips and knees were getting better since she changed to another new medication. She was really enjoying her return to teaching and was looking forward to hitting 20 years in another 2 ½ years. After lunch we returned to the doctor's office to hear about the outcome from the tests. I was sitting in the corner of the room, and the doctor was holding and feeling her hands. He called her Rosy. "Well, what do you think?" She asked. He looked at me then back to her. He asked "Rosy how long have you been teaching?" She replied, "About 17 yrs." He said, "You know, I think you need to take some time off to cool off all your joints." "Ok, we have finals, so could I at least finish the semester?" He said, "Of course." "Excellent" she replied. Then she asked him, "How long should I take off from school, they will need to know?" He said "We'll start with a year or two and go from there." Rosemary looked panicked. She asked him, "What do you mean?" He said, "I'm sorry Rosy, but...I think it's time for you to retire." Rosemary had tears in her eyes. She was only 35. Rosemary looked at me and said "I only have about a year of sick days saved up right now. After that I will probably have to go on disability."

On our way home, Rosemary started to realize a whole new chapter of her life was about to begin, and she wasn't sure she was going to like it. She worried, asking if I was going to stick with her. I remember she just cried and cried. It broke my heart. I did my best to reassure her that of course I was going to stay with her. I even joked that nobody else would have me. I told her, "We have a home together now and together we are going to stay."

Chapter 20

Learning My Craft

With Rosemary having given up her teaching she spent most of her time at home. When Rosemary bought her "dollhouse" originally, our goal was to fix up the house so it would be historically correct. This goal was easier said than done as the house had been moved several blocks to the present location back in 1925 and consequently was brutally damaged. We worked on the inside of the house for the wedding reception, and now we had to begin renovation a second time but on the outside this time. We clearly had to update it but we still needed to keep it as it was. In order to keep it original I had to learn about the style and era of the house so I visited the Lincoln Park Historical Museum.

Little did I know then that I would become very involved with the Historical Museum. I got to know those that worked for the museum as well as members of the Historical Society. One day they came knocking at my door asking if I would do a repair for them at the museum. For a year and a half, I volunteered to take care of the repairs for their new location which was the old courthouse. Eventually they outgrew that location as well so they bought the present building and asked me to be the project builder. I worked on and off at the museum for about twenty-five years. It was a place for me to go when Rosemary needed her rest. The more I worked on the museum, the better I became as a tradesman in the various fields (carpentry, plumbing, electrical, paint, masonry, etc.).

Lincoln Park Historical Museum

 I had lots of help from neighbors, friends, people from GM, and lastly, my favorite, community service volunteers referred by the court whom by doing this, were fulfilling the required community service hours (one day I hope to write a book about all that happened at the museum). I gained a great deal of respect for all the volunteers because of their willingness to learn and their dedication to the project.

 The Society, as a gesture of gratitude presented me with an enlarged, framed copy of an old photograph of the house. I used the picture as a factual basis for the renovations. We wanted to keep it historically accurate but still have it up to date. We had to install all the handicap equipment for Rosemary so she could manage on her own when I wasn't around. It took a lot of effort.

 Rosemary eventually realized a complete original restoration wasn't going to work out, so she told me to have it represent our love. At the time I had no idea what she meant and wasn't really interested in restoring it, but I promised her anyway. I understand now and am keeping that promise and redoing the house one last time. But you know what they say, third time's a charm.

When I first started to fix up the house, I didn't really want to. Rosemary was constantly nagging me and bothering me about it. I was always trying to rebel and find a way out of it. On our 5th anniversary I came home and found in the driveway a black slick beautiful 1940 Chevrolet Special Deluxe that she had seen me admiring a few months back. It had a large pink bow on it and a little card taped to the windshield that said "I love you. Get the damn house done. – Your Rosemary."

Chapter 21

My Education

One day, I was complaining to Rosemary that I couldn't identify certain things and needed help ordering products and tools for the house. She bought me a couple books and started helping me with them. It was just a short time before she realized I had a bad case of dyslexia. In my case, I wrote and read things backwards and mixed up. So she started teaching me how to compensate for the dyslexia and then homeschooled me. Within six months she proudly told me one day that I was ready to go back to high school and get my diploma. She made sure I went to adult ed. classes at Southgate High, her previous high school. I graduated in 1985. It was such a proud moment for me.

Joseph on graduation day with Buffy

Rosemary told me in order to quit being a GM factory worker and become an official licensed builder I had to first take vocational classes and instructional classes for builders.

So the time came to take the tests to determine whether or not I could receive my builder's license and become a general contractor. I had one problem, though, I couldn't read all the books fast and well enough to memorize all the laws on building standards. It was just too much. My father in law, Barney, one day asked me what the holdup was. I explained it to him. He gave me my solution. He read through ALL the books and recorded each one for me. So every day for months I would listen to all of the recordings and prepare for the test.

I took the test and got my license. It was a good day. Rosemary was proud of me too.

Chapter 22

Lions

While working at the museum, one of the members of the historical society invited me to lunch at the local Lions Club in Lincoln Park to join the Lions. It was a fantastic meeting. Everyone was friendly and the food was good. They even presented me with a certificate of appreciation for the work I had done in the community, namely the museum. I was telling Rosemary at dinner what a great group the Lions were at lunch when she mentioned to me that coincidentally she had seen a program on TV promoting the Lions in Lincoln Park. Rosemary suggested that it would be a wonderful idea for me to join. After being invited back once more the next month, I ended up joining the world's greatest service organization, Lions Clubs International, of which I have now been a Lion for 28 years.

Rosemary and I began to get more and more involved with the Lions. Within a matter of a few months, a program called Holiday Meals on Wheels had been having difficulty raising funds and finding people on the holidays to deliver all their food. Rosemary encouraged me to help out, and tried to persuade my Lions Club to get involved. They agreed. The first year a club committee organized our involvement. The members that could afford the time volunteered first but as word spread throughout the membership, more and more Lions volunteered until it became a major club project where we all enjoyed it as an activity. They are still doing it today.

Throughout my first year as a Lion I learned more about what Lions do as an international organization. Then in my second year Rosemary and I went to our first Lions Convention. I should note that Lions International is the largest service organization in the world with over 1.3 million members worldwide and since we all voluntarily belong to the same organization with the same goal of serving our community. We are just like family. At the convention, Rosemary was sitting and talking to a lady whom was involved with a Lions state project called *Welcome Home for the Blind*. Rosemary thought that was so neat and expressed to me that we should get involved. The project was so dear to me that I eventually became a member of the Advisory Board which I immensely enjoyed.

Lions also have a foreign exchange program in which Rosemary and I had become very involved by hosting exchanged students. We hosted 16 children in total from all around the world over the years. It felt like we had adopted them as our own. Even though they only stayed three to six months, they became part of our family forever. Each one was an incredible experience, and we now had a big family. Rosemary loved being their mother especially since we were never going to be able to have any children of our own. They shared their culture with us, their different and unique varieties of authentic food. In addition each student brought their own traditions and values with them and we combined them with ours so they wouldn't lose sight of home while embracing new experiences.

Lion Joseph P. Griggs

One time, we had a sweet, petite Japanese girl stay with us. Problems occurred- Growing pains. Apparently I spoke too loud and I scared her because she always thought I was angry because her father was a very soft-spoken man. We called her parents and they explained to her not to worry and to me that I could not speak so loudly in front of her because it would make her nervous. After that misunderstanding was solved we ended up being a very close family; however, she always seemed to like Rosemary more than me, but that's ok.

Three local projects where we were very involved were Penrickton Center for Blind Children, Leader Dogs for the Blind, and Beaumont Silent Children Fund.

Penrickton's mission statement neatly sums up the magnificent organization as:

"a unique, private non-profit agency, providing five-day residential, day care, and consultation/evaluation services to blind, multi-disabled children ages one through twelve. Each program is individually designed to promote independence in all aspects of daily living. Penrickton Center utilizes its experience and expertise to train and serve families, children and professionals through support services, education and advocacy".

Leader Dogs for the Blind:

"enhances the lives of blind and visually impaired through empowering people who are blind or visually impaired with lifelong skills for independent travel through quality Leader Dogs, highly effective client instruction and innovative services. In addition to their guide dog program, they offer other programs that enhance a person's including orientation and mobility training, GPS training, and seminars for Orientation and Mobility professionals. Currently, Leader Dog is the only facility in the Western Hemisphere to teach Deaf-Blind students to work with a guide dog."

Beaumont Silent Children Fund:

"is a Lions fund to support Beaumont's Center for Childhood Speech and Language Disorders was established in 1972 to help children with speech and language disorders to communicate. As one of the largest hospital-based children's speech and language centers in the United States, they provide a variety of specialty care programs for children with speech and language disorders."

The Lions rescued our marriage. Lions, along with the church, became a stress reliever for Rosemary and me. Helping others who may not be able to help themselves was a great distraction for us when it came to Rosemary's illness. I strongly recommend to anybody who reads this book to visit their local Lions Club. It pulled us out of the rut and helped us bond. Rosemary personally ran the Answering Service for all the clubs in our District. She had done that up to the last year of her life. She loved to talk to people and help them find a club that could help with a solution or information that could take care of their needs. The Lions gave me a new purpose in life while giving me a breather by allowing Rosemary another "outlet" (as she put it) to reduce her burden on me, and now she had a new social circle where she could speak to and interact with others. Rosemary did plenty of lions work but never officially became one until 1996, 10 years after me. The funny thing was she was doing most

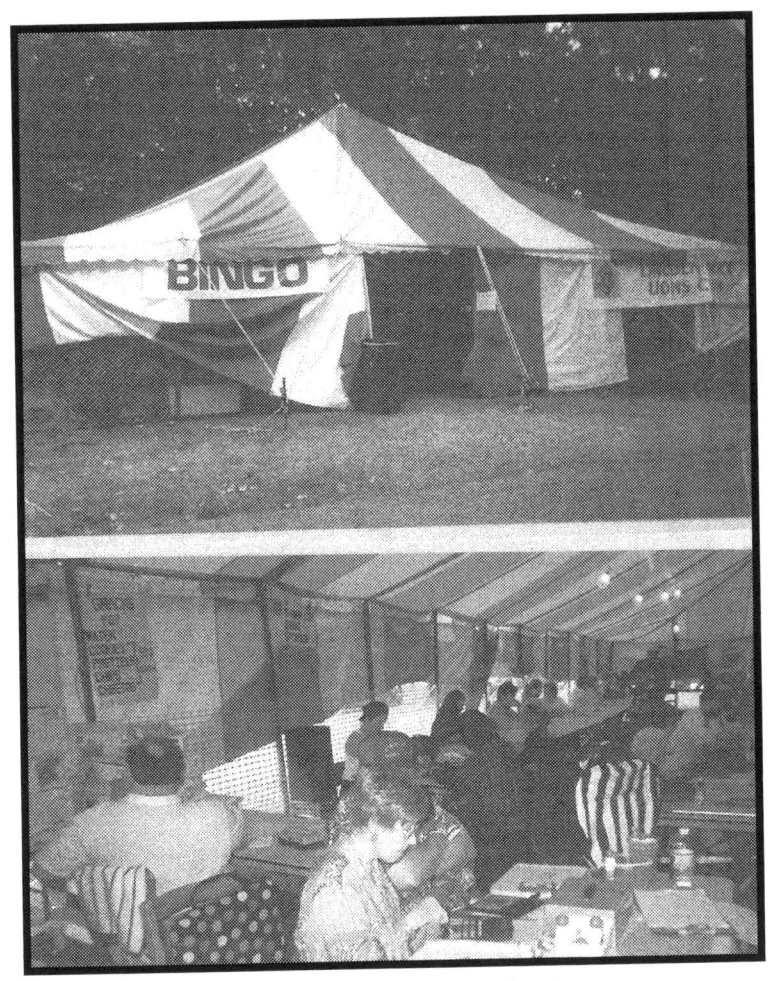

Lincoln Park Lions Fundraiser

of the secretary and committee work before she even became a member; she loved doing the newsletter. She swore that she wouldn't stop working and was determined to become a member when the gender barrier was broken. Eventually she

Lion Joseph P. Griggs

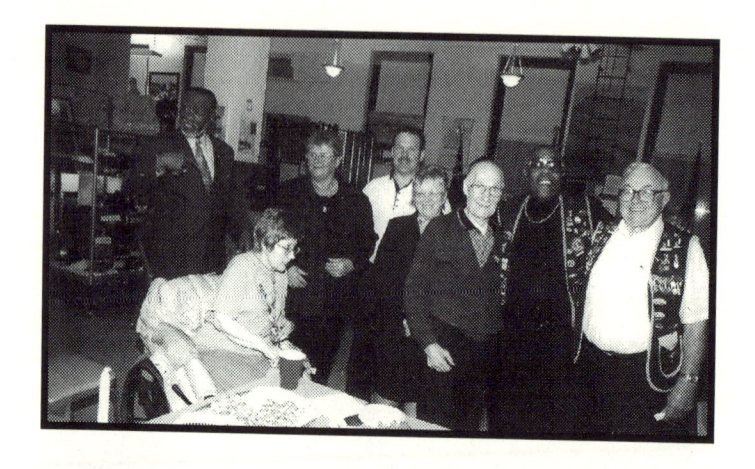

Rosemary volunteering with the Lions

was sworn in as a Lion at the convention by the District Governor himself. It was a big honor!

Although being a bit of a ruffian when I was younger, joining Lions taught me maturity and leadership skills. I realized helping others was my true calling and it felt wonderful. To this day Lions still plays a giant role in my life. I don't know where I would be without them. For as long as I can remember this had been the best part of Rosemary's life. It's still the best part of mine. Our favorite part about being Lions was being together and serving together. Thank you to all the members, family, and friends out there for supporting our efforts over time.

Chapter 23

Rosemary's Power

As I dove deeper and deeper into Lions, I found myself chairing many different projects over time including being president of my own club for 5 years. I was on several different boards, and at the time the list just seemed to go on. I was asked to work on the 2004 international convention so I became the chair for the communications for everyone in the whole convention. I asked my fellow Lion, Leo Buk to co-chair it with me and he agreed. Over time I became close with his wife, Vicky also and she found out Rosemary was home alone and needed help. So she offered to take care of Rosemary and the house, word for word - "ESPECIALLY *the lady stuff*" and they became very good friends. It worked out great.

Some of the past Lions Governors put it in my head that I should run for Vice District Governor and thereafter District Governor for our area. What got their attention was around that time I set up a few training seminars for Guiding Lions (new club advisors), including my best buddy, John. So by the time I finally decided to run I had already been Lions'

Lion Joseph P. Griggs

Region and Zone Chair twice and I was ready. So the time came for me to give my speech about running for Vice District Governor. I worked on it for over a month. It was finally ready. I had just started to launch my campaign. Everything was going perfectly until the cabinet meeting. It was my time to shine. I confidently marched to the podium, looked around at the crowd with my wide charming smile (if I do say so myself) and I straightened and organized my papers, took my time and began to give my first official campaign speech.

Joseph running for District Governor

I had just introduced myself when someone walked up to the podium and stopped me in the middle of everything with all eyes on us. And he whispered to me, "Your wife is upset and crying you need to go to her, NOW." I glanced at the crowd then excused myself and went to Rosemary. She was inside a cluster of concerned people balling her eyes out. I awkwardly sat down next to her; my face was probably beet red. So many people were watching and listening. I said, "Rosemary, what is going on?" "Don't run!" she responded. "Why? Why are you doing this now?! You've known I have been wanting to run for a long time now?" "Please don't run, please don't, not now, not at this time," she continued. "What's wrong with now?!" I protested. "Just give me one year, that's all I'm begging for, please." She pleaded. "Please, just one more year..." I just gawked at her and shook my head in astonishment. "Well, who would run in my place?" I asked. Some Lions chirped in and said, "Joseph, it's just a year it's not that long." I looked at them then I looked back and said to Rosemary, "Well, if not me then who the heck is gonna run?" Rosemary patted at her red puffy eyes and pointed directly across the table to my friend, Herb Worthy. And she said, "You and Herb have done everything together; you both qualify. He will take your place."

I relented.

I trudged Herb up to the podium, announced my withdrawal from the race and excused myself. Herb took over with an improvisation speech while

Lion Herb Worthy

I didn't utter another word for the rest of the night.

The next day I told Rosemary I hoped I'd be able to run as Herb's Vice District Governor next year.

Joseph and Herb Worthy of Ecorse Park Lions

Herb and Roberta Worthy

Chapter 24

Fading Health

Not long after conceding to Rosemary's wish that I put off running for the Lion's top office in my area I came to know that Rosemary was not going to ever truly bounce back and her body was not going to stop deteriorating, slowly and painfully. She had a beautiful mind and a great way with people. Everything was worsening, her muscles, bones, joints, everything. It had gotten to the point where it was hard for her to talk because it was too painful and hard to work the muscles in her jaw. I realized her drive to continue living was me and only me. For the rest of her life, she focused on helping me become successful. I was her last student. She used to tease me that she was only sticking around just to see what I was going to do next. The more time went by, the more I understood that she was right by holding off the election; we had so many doctors' appointments, so many decisions, so many surgeries that had to be made and done. More importantly, we had to spend what little time we had left together, sharing each other's company. The doctors were considering replacing both her shoulders and elbows because the cartilage was all gone. They decided that they would allow her ankles to fuse in place. She would basically stay in a wheelchair for the rest of her life. She refused to give up, though; she would occasionally shuffle around almost walking like a penguin. Her hands and feet started breaking down again and they would need to replace them for the third time. The doctor asked Rosemary to step out. The doctor told me she had been on heavy, heavy medication since she was 9 up until now in her early fifties. The doctor put his arm around me and said, "Joseph, Rosemary is living just for you." Somebody said out loud what I had been wondering about for too long. I didn't know what to say or how to respond. But I did know I was so thankful for having Rosemary in my life. I think the doctor was trying to hint at me that the end was near but I knew Rosemary had been warning me too. Eventually we became more desperate and the medicines became more extreme and experimental. I had to administer a shot into her stomach every day from then on.

She practically had little to no control of her body. She lost weight ridiculously fast. We moved her bed to the main floor because she couldn't get upstairs and she slept there alone because I couldn't take the sound of her bones grinding as she moved. It was extremely eerie.

What hurt her most was the emotional toll it had taken on me. I tried my hardest not to show a single tear as I watched my wife of 23 years crumble away right before my very eyes knowing I could not stop the inevitable but she knew that I was breaking. This is partially why I spent all those years at the museum as a volunteer so that Rosemary would never see me cry and that I could escape next door and fortify my emotions and still be close enough to make sure she was alright.

With Rosemary's health as it was, I just couldn't keep working and taking care of her at the same time. Her care was a full time job and if anybody was going to do it, it was going to be me. I went to my boss at General Motors and gave my resignation; my 30 year career at GM was over. My job now was to care for Rosemary and her fading health.

CHAPTER 25

Our Pets
(Rosemary's babies)

To help watch over Rosemary when I wasn't around, we kept a few pets. Over time we had one bird, one hamster, two cats, and three dogs.

Lion Joseph P. Griggs

My personal favorite was my blue boy bird named Suzie. He was a blast. Every Friday, my boys would come over to play poker at my house and my canary would fly around and sip at the guys beers so eventually he just got his own cup and every Friday my poor bird got wasted. I should've taken him to AAB (alcoholics anonymous for birds). He should have been the poster child. Sadly though, one day he flew out the window. It was the last time I ever saw him. I bet he went to the bar two blocks away.

We also had Biscuit, the terrier and Bosco, the black lab who were the terrible duo. Biscuit was the little devil himself and poor Bosco was his overseer and did his best to make sure he stayed out of trouble. Trouble found them one day while the postal service was having a dedication ceremony after having installed a new drive-up mailbox right across the street. Coincidentally, our brand new mailman, first day on the job and probably the last, strolled up to my house at the same time. My front door was open and the new mailman saw me through the screen. He waved his hand with the package and hollered "PACKAGE!" My littler Biscuit took flight like a bat out of hell. He busted right through the screen door on a physical rampage with Bosco right on his tail. I came running out the door screaming "DON'T RUN!" The first thing that man did was run

Kissed by My Confidant

for his life. Poor Biscuit ran and ripped the poor mailman's pants clean off in the middle of the street right in front of the postmaster and all the neighbors. It was a nightmare.

All our pets have since passed except one, the she devil in fur, Rosemary's queen of the house Ariel, Rosemary's last pet. And the cat knows that I can't do *nothing* to her so she makes my life miserable.

Chapter 26

Her Time

Imagine how it would feel being a prisoner in your own body. You know you're dying; you know you will die. Every day you fight but can't help wondering, today, tomorrow? When? Every bone in your body is always breaking down, crumbling, and there is no cure. Eventually few bones in your body are actually yours, each, another piece inserted by doctors, never to last long enough. You wonder, "Why me?" Some days you spend looking for the silver lining but most are spent with your heart twisted and lurched in knots trying to squeeze out any hope you have left. There is but one anchor in your life, the antidote to your never ending pain. Always in reach but never enough. The one day it truly must save you, you've run out. Nowhere to be found. Hope has run dry, you make the decision. You close your eyes to rest. It's over.

The days started flying and seemed to blend together. The more time went by, the less Rosemary was able to do on her own. She began constantly calling either one of our mothers or Leo's wife, Vicky. Vicky would bring food to Rosemary while a few of our other friends as well as people from the museum would drop off food baskets to her as they stopped in to check on her when I wasn't around.

I had to start making additional money to supplement the bills because my retirement was not enough. I was and still am a licensed residential builder so it was easy for me to find odd jobs to earn extra money to pay for Rosemary's help, medicine, and doctor bills. Often, though, it was quite frustrating. I figured if I could just start my own business, I would be able to be home and have other people work for me but Rosemary was afraid of the risk of the business failing and there was too much at stake to risk us losing everything.

One day, I got a call from Lion Al Cherelli from the Cherelli's Market down the street from the house. There was a problem with one of the refrigerators so I went down to fix it. I was familiar with their equipment and knew it wouldn't take me more than an hour so I made Rosemary's breakfast and set it down next to the bed. I'm not exactly sure how long I was gone but I do know that all of a sudden I had a strange, horrible feeling come over me that something was wrong. Al came over and asked if I could do another job for him and I told him I needed to check on Rosemary and I'd come right back.

When I walked back into the house I noticed that the food was cold and untouched. Rosemary was staring straight up at the ceiling. She looked like she was turning blue. I laid my hand over her mouth and I couldn't feel any breath but she grabbed my arm slightly. I rushed to call 911. The fire department came right over in no time. Eventually four firefighters, paramedics, an ambulance, and three police cars showed up in total. One officer took me by the shoulder and sat me down on the porch to keep me calm while they focused on her condition. As I sat there dazed, I asked why I couldn't be with her. He told me it was just protocol to make sure there was no foul play at hand. Then time stopped. It seemed like everything was moving so fast around me but I sat frozen. I noticed a crowd had gathered on my front lawn, even Al had rushed over worriedly from the market. All were concerned and wanted to know if they could help in any way.

At last, a paramedic came out to speak to me on the porch along with two policemen. As I stood there speechless, they asked me if I wanted to resuscitate her. The words roared out on their own, "Yes! Yes! At least try!" And time froze for me once again.

Lion Joseph P. Griggs

    I don't know how much time passed. It seemed like forever. They came out again and one of the officers stepped forward and asked me, "Joseph, where do you want her?" I named off every hospital in the area I didn't care where or how much it would take. I just wanted my Rosemary to be ok. "I don't think you understand, Joseph, she's gone."

    I was momentarily quiet. Dumbfounded. I said, "Take her to Ray Alex Funeral Home, two blocks from my house." It was the second time in my life that I watched them close the zipper over the face of someone I cared about; the first was my father and now my Rosemary.

Chapter 27

The Love I Have Lost

Once the ambulance took Rosemary away, everyone who had showed up began to leave. My dear friend, Lion Herb Worthy pulled up and said "Joseph, you need to get out of here. If you want to go and get a drink to numb the pain, let's do it. We can go anywhere, whatever you wanna do." As I got in the car I told him no, I didn't want anything to drink. He closed the car door and said go ahead and cry. We drove all the way to Ohio and back.

That was the worst night of my life. The calls started pouring in. I didn't know what or how to say anything to them. I found myself getting angry because I wasn't ready for Rosemary to leave me yet. I realized how much I depended on her despite how sick she was. I missed her. Just waking up in the morning I needed her. That day I lost my best friend, my lover, and my confidant.

In the morning I went to the funeral home to make the arrangements. I brought Rosemary's favorite dress from when she taught school that she used to love to wear. I knew she would have liked that. I asked her sister Susan to accompany me to the funeral home so we could make the arrangements together. We picked out the casket which was baby blue inside. We located her plot and I bought one for myself next to hers so when I die I will be laid to rest along side of her. I also ordered her headstone, which was inscribed with, "Rosemary, Wife of Joseph May 4, 1951 – November 13, 2006."

The next day was visitation. So many people from the museum, her work, her school, Lions, friends, family, students, and neighbors came. It seemed people from all four corners of the earth showed up to pay their respects. Everyone had a place in their heart for Rosemary.

The day of the funeral was a dream to me, all a blur. I don't remember much. The little I do remember was the tons of people and a lot of pretty flowers at the funeral home. It was so beautiful but I didn't stay. Near the end, a relative came up to me and started asking me about Rosemary's life insurance money- asking for a loan right there at the funeral. Rosemary hadn't even gone in the ground yet. I went blind with rage. I walked out and never looked back.

Everything Rosemary owned, I gave away to charity. Everything. I couldn't bear to see anyone around brandish her belongings. It would make me cry, tearing and shredding my heart.

I've never felt so empty. It was like someone took my heart and ripped it out of my chest, as if I would have to go on living without feeling, without a part of my soul. I felt nothing but pain and grief. I have never loved another woman as much as I ever loved Rosemary. I wonder now if someone, someday may help to fill that hole which she left so I can fulfill at least one more promise to the love I have lost.

Rosemary, I know that you're with me in my heart and in Heaven. Your mother told me before she died that you are going to send me an angel to help fill that awful, dark hole. Thanks Rosemary, I will always love you forever and a day.

Chapter 28

The Ten Promises

In the months before her health took its final toll, to show Rosemary how special she was to me, we would have 'dates.' Since she couldn't leave the house we would make backdrops on a blanket and hang it up behind her bed. For example, one time we went to Hawaii. I got a giant sheet and painted it blue with white clouds then I got her a lei which is a traditional Hawaiian flower necklace. We had Hawaiian music in the background and I cooked us up a Hawaiian feast. It was fun. We picnicked and had dates in Hungary, Greece, Poland, and such all the time. She would prepare the date and plan everything for me to do. "Post it" notes littered our household. Usually the day before our dates I would take her to her mothers and her mother would do her hair for our dates. Although after these dates it would take Rosemary almost a week to recover, it was our way of staying connected and I loved how happy it made Rosemary.

Usually, after these dates, just before Rosemary would go to bed, she would have me make her promises. She would always start by saying, "You know, Joseph, you need to make me some promises in case something should happen to me." These were my promises to her:

{} Promise # 1

"Don't be alone when I've passed. Find someone for yourself, you're not the kind of man who should live alone. You need someone to love you."

{X} Promise # 2

She was very concerned that we wouldn't complete the Lincoln Park Lions Park that we had been working on for so long. "It was designed for all the residents to use but especially the handicapped, so see it to that it is finished."

{X} Promise # 3

"Slow down at the museum. Take a break and start your life back up again. Let someone else do all the work. She felt I had done my share for them and it was time to move on.

{X} Promise # 4

"Get the damn house done, but please Joseph make the house... you. Not what they want, not what the city wants, not what history wants. No. They didn't pay for it, I did, and it's for you to learn how to fix things on. Make it for yourself. I know you will.

{X} Promise # 5

"Please take care of yourself, stay in good health, and don't think hard about it, just do what the doctor says."

{X} Promise # 6

"When I'm gone please slow down. You don't have to do everything. Don't work so hard that you don't get to see the world and enjoy it."

{X} Promise # 7

"The trips we never got to take like our honeymoon - travel there for me. I will be with you in spirit." I went to Hawaii alone and I brought some of her personal things and a lei. I found a place by one of the Catholic churches by the ocean. I cast it all into the water and said the Lord's Prayer.

{X} Promise # 8

"Promise that you will check in on my mother, and be helpful to her after I've passed." I usually visited her mother on Sundays or called to check on her until she died.

{} Promise # 9

"Fulfill our dream, and go to Paris and find the lady in the red dress. You'll be an artist painting in the street, the young lady will pretend to be a lady of the night and she will come up to you take your arm and you will find some little nice place. Play the song *The Lady in Red* and have her dance for you, just one more time for you."

{} Promise # 10

The "Last Kiss" is the one thing that Rosemary asked for that I will never be able to do. She talked about it all the time. Some nights when she was worried she wouldn't make it through the night, she would give me a very long slow and meaningful kiss. When I received kisses like this I knew she was worried. The thing Rosemary loved to do most was to kiss me. Goodbye, Hello, Good morning, Good night, Good afternoon, you name it. I got a kiss for it. There was never a day that went by where she didn't tell me she loved me more than at least five times. The last kiss was the biggest promise I made Rosemary that I could never keep. "Kiss me right before I die so my last breath would be yours." Sadly, the police and paramedics forced me to wait on the porch while the medical team attended to her at the end and I was unable to fulfill my promise.

Chapter 29

Epilogue

A month before Rosemary died, I decided that I wanted to get our wedding blessed so I went to our Catholic priest, and I asked him to bless our wedding, he told me he couldn't unless I became Catholic and then he could bless our wedding the very next day. So, I made it my mission to become Catholic. I went home and told Rosemary.

The next day she came to the interview with me and there they asked me to tell them three things about what I liked and disliked about the Catholic Church. "That's easy, what I like about it is that I like the costumes, I know how long the sermons are gonna be every time, and the free wine. What I don't like about the Catholic Church is, praying so much to Mary when it should be to God, why there are so many saints, and confession because I don't wanna tell nobody my business." Rosemary just rolled her eyes and shook her head.

Sadly, Rosemary died before she could see my transformation. Once a week I went to class to learn what I needed to know to become Catholic. It was awkward because I had to undergo my education with a bunch of

Lion Joseph P. Griggs

young kids. I always felt so out of place, but now when I look back it was darn hilarious because it was big 'ol me with lil 'ol them. We finished class the following Easter and had our admittance into the Catholic Church shortly after. I stood in dead center with my red face and eight kids on both sides of me. We received our certificates and I knew I was in. Many people came for me that night and many tears were shed. They all knew I did this for Rosemary and were all proud of me. She was there with me on that stage in spirit and I could feel her smiling down on me. It was a very special night. I felt Rosemary with me again. I know she is always with me, My Confidant.

We Are Lions

We meet the needs of our local communities and the world.

Our 1.35 million men and women in over 200 countries and geographic areas conduct vision and health screenings, build parks, support eye hospitals, award scholarships, assist youth, and provide help in time of disaster and much more.

Join us in making our communities and
the world better places to live.

LIONS CLUBS INTERNATIONAL
HEADQUARTERS
300 W 22nd ST
Oak Brook, IL 60523-8842
(630) 571-5466 - (630) 571-8890 Fax
Web: www.lionsclubs.org   E-mail: lions@lionsclubs.org

Lions of Michigan State Office

EXECUTIVE DIRECTOR
5730 Executive Drive
(517) 887-6640

Wendy Burns
Lansing, MI 48911
(517) 887-6642 Fax
wburns@lionsofmi.com

Web: www.lionsofmi.com - Email: lions@lionsofmi.com

State Treasurer
30752 Glenwood Circle
(586) 776-7243 Res

Paul Hemeryck
Warren, MI, 48088
(586) 774-0440 Bus

Email: hemeryck@ameritec.net

Organization & Projects

* = District Project   **= State/ Multiple District Project

** Lions of Michigan Service Foundation
(517) 887-6640
(517) 887-6642 Fax

Chad McCann Executive Administrator
5730 Executive Drive
Lansing, MI 48911
Email: chadmccann@kmcmail.net

Web: www.lmsf.net   Email: lionsfoundation@kmcmail.net

* Beaumont Silent Children's Fund
(248) 691-4777 Bus
(248) 691-4710 Fax

Michael Rolnick PhD, Director
3601 W. Thirteen Mile Rd.
Royal Oak, MI 48073

Web: www.beaumont.edu/speech
Kris Rutkowski, Supervisor

Detroit Radio Information Service (DRIS)
Ron Jones (313) 577-4255 Bus
(313) 577-1300 Fax

Ron Jones
4600 Cass Ave.
Detroit, MI 48201

Web: www.dris.org   E-mail:dris@wayne.edu

Greater Detroit Agency for the Blind G.D.A.B.V.I.
(313) 272-3900 Bus
(313) 272-6893 Fax

Victor A Arbulu
16625 Grand River Ave.
Detroit, MI 48227

Web: www.gdabvi.org   Email: info@gdabvi.org

** Leader Dogs for the Blind
(248) 651-9011 Bus
(248) 651-5912 Fax

Sue Daniels President & CEO
1038 S. Rochester Rd.
Rochester Hills, MI 48307

Web: www.leaderdog.org   Email: leaderdog@leaderdog.org
Toll free: (888) 777-5332

* LIONS HEARING CENTER OF MICHIGAN (888) 542-6424	Phil Wells 4201 St. Antoine, 5E-UHC Detroit, MI 48201

Web: www.lhcmi.org Email: pwells@med.wayne.edu
Wayne State University & Detroit Medical Center

** BEAR LAKE (LIONS VISUALLY IMPAIRED YOUTH CAMP) (810) 245-0726 (810) 245-0750 Fax	Dennis Tomkins Director 3409 N. Five Lakes Road Lapeer, MI 48446

Web: bearlakecamp.org Email: bearlakecamp@tir.com

MADONNA UNIVERSITY/LIONS HEARING PROGRAM (734) 432-5315 Bus (734) 432-5333 Fax	Sister Rose Marie Kujawa President 36600 Schoolcraft Rd. Livonia, MI 48150-1176

Web: www.madonna.edu Email: srosemarie@madonna.edu

** MICHIGAN EYE BANK (800) 247-7250 Bus (734) 780-2143 Fax	Lisa Langley Executive Director 4889 Venture Ave. Ann Arbor, MI 48108

Web: www.midwesteyebanks.org E-mail: info@midwesteyebanks.org
Illinois - Michigan - New Jersey

* PENRICKTON CENTER FOR BLIND CHILDREN (734) 946-7500 Bus (734) 946-6707 Fax	Kurt Sebaly 26530 Eureka Rd. Taylor, MI 48180

Web: www.penrickton.com

PROJECT KID SIGHT (517) 887-6640 Bus (517) 887-6642 Fax	Chad McCann Executive Administrator Project Kid Sight c/o Lions of Michigan Foundation 5730 Executive Drive, Lansing MI 48911

Southgate Zodiac Racquet & Health Club, 14795 Dix-Toledo Rd., Southgate, MI 48195	Club# 4465 Region: 3 Zone: 1 12/2/1957 1st & 3rd Tuesday 6:30 PM

Dates to Remember

2015 Lions International Convention	**June 26-30th, 2015** - Honolulu, Hawaii
11-A1 1st Cabinet Meeting	**July 23, 2015** - Westfield Community Center Trenton
2015 USA/Canada Forum	**September 17-19th, 2015** - Grand Rapids, MI
MD 11 Convention	**May 15 -16, 2016** - Best Western, Sterling Heights, MI
2016 Lions International Convention	**June 24-28th, 2016** - Fukuoka, Japan
2016 USA/Canada Forum	**September, 2016** - Ohama, Nebraska
2017 Lions International Convention	**June 30-July 4, 2017** - Chicago, Illinois
2018 Lions International Convention	**June 29th- July 3rd, 2018** - Las Vegas, NV
2019 Lions International Convention	**July 5-9th, 2019** - Milan, Italy

Lions International Purposes

- **To Organize**, charter and supervise service clubs to be known as Lions clubs.
- **To Coordinate** the activities and standardize the administration of Lions clubs.
- **To Create** and foster a spirit of understanding among the peoples of the world.
- **To Promote** the principles of good government and good citizenship.
- **To Take** an active interest in the civic, cultural, social and moral welfare of the community.
- **To Unite** the clubs in the bonds of friendship, good fellowship and mutual understanding.
- **To Provide** a forum for the open discussion of all matters of public interest; provided, however, that partisan politics and sectarian religion shall not be debated by club members.

- **To Encourage** service-minded people to serve their community without personal financial reward, and to encourage efficiency and promote high ethical standards in commerce, industry, professions, public works and private endeavors.

Lions Code of Ethics

- **To Show** my faith in the worthiness of my vocation by industrious application to the end that I may merit a reputation for quality of service.
- **To Seek** success and to demand all fair remuneration or profit as my just due, but to accept no profit or success at the price of my own self-respect lost because of unfair advantage taken or because of questionable acts on my part.
- **To Remember** that in building up my business it is not necessary to tear down another's; to be loyal to my clients or customers and true to myself.
- **Whenever** a doubt arises as to the right or ethics of my position or action towards others, to resolve such doubt against myself.
- **To Hold** friendship as an end and not a means. To hold that true friendship exists not on account of the service performed by one another, but that true friendship demands nothing but accepts service in the spirit in which it is given.
- **Always** to bear in mind my obligations as a citizen to my nation, my state, and my community, as to give them my unswerving loyalty in word, act, and deed. To give them freely of my time, labor and means.
- **To Aid** others by giving my sympathy to those in distress, my aid to the weak, and my substance to the needy.
- **To Be Careful** with my criticism and liberal with my praise; to build up and not destroy.

· Mission Statement

· To create and foster a spirit of understanding among all people

- for humanitarian needs by providing voluntary services
- through community involvement and international cooperation.

- **The Parting Words**

- **The pleasure of our fellowship reluctantly we end. Although our paths now grow apart, our hearts in friendship blend. Although we go our separate ways, this pledge we shall maintain, that we shall live as Lions should until we meet again.**

"CELEBRATING THE BIRTHPLACE OF Lions Clubs International"

On June 7, 1917 at the LaSalle Hotel in Chicago Illinois, a meeting of practical-minded visionaries met and set the stage for the organization and later that year in Dallas Texas, of today's international association. Minutes of that meeting show it had been organized by Melvin Jones, a Chicago insurance man. The minutes also would show that Dr. William Woods, an Evansville, Indiana physician was listed as President, International Association of Lions Clubs.

The first club chartered was the Chicago (central) Lions Club on August 2, 1917.

Cutting across all national, racial, and cultural boundaries, Lions Clubs International activities included:

*Sight conservation and work with the blind
*Hearing conservation and work with the deaf
*Citizenship, educational, health, and social services
*Drug education and prevention programs
*Diabetes detection and research

* Work for international cooperation and understanding, including international youth camp and youth exchange programs

Moving forward, clubs were chartered in Michigan, the Marquette and Grand Rapids clubs were chartered in 1919 and later the Downtown Detroit Lions Club was chartered. The significance of this led to the gathering of Lions from the Detroit club with prospective Lions from Ontario, Canada from the other side of the Detroit River. On March 12, 1920 the Border Cities Lions Club was established consisting of communities of Ford, Walkerville, Windsor, Sandwich, and Ojibway (later named Windsor Lions Club).

From those early days with 6,451 members, 113 clubs in 2 nations we now record over 1.35 million members, in over 45,000 clubs in 209 countries and geographic areas.

AS 2020 APPROACHES, WE PLAN TO ACKNOWLEDGE THE 100 YEAR ANNIVERSARY OF THE BIRTHPLACE OF LIONS CLUBS INTERNATIONAL BY ERECTING LION MONUMENTS ON BOTH SIDES OF THE DETROIT RIVER.

A PORTION OF THE NET SALES OF THIS PUBLICATION WILL GO TO THE MONUMENT FUND.

FOR THOSE WISHING TO DONATE TO THE MONUMENT FUND.

MAIL DONATIONS TO:

LIONS OF MICHIGAN SERVICE FOUNDATION, C/O 100YR MONUMENT FUND, 5730 EXECUTIVE DR. LANSING MI 48911

THE HISTORY WAS EXCERPTED FROM "WE SERVE-A HISTORY OF THE LIONS CLUBS" BY LION RICHARD MARTIN, REGENCY GATEWAY, WASHINGTON D.C., DISTRIBUTED BY NATIONAL BOOK NETWORK, LANHAM, MD, PRINTED IN 1991. COPYRIGHT EXCLUDES MAGAZINES (PAPERBACKS).

Printed in the United States
By Bookmasters